COOKING WITH A DAN

COOKING WITH A DANISH FLAVOUR presents nearly 250 tempting ideas for both everyday meals and entertaining. The ingredients required for cooking in the Danish way are not so very different to our own; it is the endlessly imaginative and colourful way in which Danish cooks combine everyday foodstuffs which gives the dishes their characteristic stamp. Many of the recipes are built around the bacon, butter and cheese for which the Danish farmers are justly famed. There is an entire chapter devoted to bacon cookery – unique to Britain, and wonderfully economical and versatile – and special sections on making *smørrebrød,* the festive open sandwiches which are so popular in Denmark, and arranging a Cold Table. From soups and starters through meat, fish and poultry to desserts and the incomparable Danish pastries, the recipes included here will introduce a whole new range into your kitchen repertory. Illustrated throughout in full colour, this book is the definitive guide to cooking in the Danish way, and to presenting your meals in the colourful, eye-catching manner so expertly practised in Denmark.

Cooking with a
Danish Flavour

Pauline Viola & Knud Ravnkilde

Elm Tree Books · London

Mycella Party Pieces (page 82)

First published in Great Britain 1978
by Elm Tree Books/Hamish Hamilton Ltd
27 Wrights Lane, London W8 5TZ
Reprinted 1983, 1986.

Copyright © 1978 by Pauline Viola and Knud Ravnkilde

Design and layout by Logos Design, Windsor
Set in Monophoto Apollo

Line drawings by Pamela Dawson

Printed in Spain by Mateu Cromo
Artes Gráficas, S.A., Madrid

ISBN 0 241 1231 X

Note on the measurements

Ingredients are given in both metric and imperial (in brackets) measures and the recipes are written to produce successful results regardless of which method you choose to use. Follow one column or the other. *Do not* try to make comparisons between the two because they are not exact conversions.

In general, metric measures for solid foods are based on a unit of 25 grammes. On this basis, the pound equivalent of 450g has been used, except in the case of weighed-out foods such as meat, fish and fresh vegetables, which will usually be bought in units of 0.5kg (500g). For liquid ingredients, 600ml has been used for 1 pint, and 1 litre for $1\frac{3}{4}$ pints. British standard metric measuring spoons have been used for small quantities of both liquids and solids, and in all cases the spoon measures are level.

Contents

Introduction

This book is dedicated to the cooks of many lands, wherever Danish food and an interest in the Danish way of life are to be found. It is a book of modern recipes for dishes eaten in Danish homes today rather than those cooked and served a hundred years ago, although many old favourites remain.

Ranging from the delights of *smørrebrød* and *Wienerbrød* to the ubiquitous *frikadeller*, meat, fish and desserts, Danish baking and the Cold Table, there are nearly 250 recipes and ideas which are practical and easy to follow. The ingredients required are not so very different to our own. It is how they are used that is different and that makes the finished dish so interesting and original to the newcomer.

Many of the dishes included here feature the pride of the Danish food producers, their famous Danish bacon, butter and cheese. These staple foods have been brought to a peak of quality through a long tradition of producing the best by an élite group of men and women. Working together through an agricultural co-operative movement at first small but now producing food for export to over a hundred countries, they have become an example of proficiency and success to farmers everywhere.

The ways in which people of other lands use these quality foods in their own homes has also been a source of inspiration for this book, especially in the section on bacon cookery, which is unique to Britain. There are similarities, too, with the foods of Denmark's Scandinavian and other European neighbours, and Danes travelling abroad on holiday continue to bring back many new ideas. But these influences are all dominated by the Danish cuisine itself. This retains its age-old peasant thriftiness, making use of every scrap of food in the most economical and tasty way, and combines food preparation with a style of presentation which seems to stem from the character of the people themselves.

The Danish way with food has much to recommend it and fortunately there is little need for special equipment in its preparation. An inexpensive ring mould is useful because Danish cooks often use one to give a particular finish to a party dish. They use their mincers a lot and every Danish household has a heavy saucepan suitable for pot roasting. These are really quite ordinary items which can be purchased nearly everywhere if necessary, and only a few recipes require them.

Little ball-shaped pancakes called *aebleskiver*, which do require a special pan for which no substitute could be found, have reluctantly been omitted. So have *crustader* as few people today, including Danes, have the necessary *crustade* iron to make these deep-fried pastry cases. And *øllebrød*, the famous beer 'porridge', cannot be made without the authentic rye bread and non-alcoholic beer which are seldom available outside Denmark. No such problem arises, though, with the cooking fats – Danish butter and lard – or the Danish cheeses which are exported all over the world.

With a few exceptions, herbs and spices in the Danish kitchen are much the same as in Britain. The main difference is in the frequent use of dill which lends a unique flavour to many dishes, as do allspice

Danish Pastries – *Wienerbrød* (page 103)

and cardamom among the spices. All three are available here, although sometimes they must be searched for.

In a dairy country like Denmark, it is no surprise to find that an unusual variety of milk products feature in sauces and desserts – fresh cream, soured cream, yoghurt, *ymer*, which is similar to yoghurt, and buttermilk. Only fresh and soured cream, yoghurt and buttermilk have been used in these recipes as *ymer* is unobtainable outside Denmark.

People with fine palates often notice the distinctive flavour in mayonnaise and salads which comes from the Danish vinegar. Known as Heidelberg vinegar, it is pale in colour with a delicate sweet-sour flavour; recipes where it would be used have been adjusted to come as near as possible to the original flavour.

Salting meat and fish and making sausages are, alas, two branches of Danish cooking which have had to be omitted for lack of space.

Danish cuisine is distinctive, exciting, and yet practical, too. With a little thought, and very little extra time, all the ideas in this book can be presented at the table in the colourful, eye-catching way so expertly practised in Denmark.

Danish Cuisine and Customs

The most frequent description of a Danish meal is 'plentiful and festive' but behind present-day lavishness lies a story of need, of having to make much out of little. Since the Middle Ages this small country across the North Sea has been known as a farming and seafaring community. With no mineral wealth under its gently rolling countryside, Denmark had to make the most out of the soil and early developed a reliance on livestock and the export of dairy produce to sustain the country's economy.

The story of Danish cookery has been flavoured not only by the farmers' way of life but also by the church and by royalty, as befits this oldest monarchy in Europe. Denmark was a Catholic nation until the Reformation and very high church until about a hundred years ago. For centuries the Church insisted on four meatless days each week. So rigid was this edict that it was included in the court orders of King Christian II in the sixteenth century, although those orders did not dictate the same standards for everyone. Courtiers were allowed six courses for dinner; the King had ten. On meat days only the King and Queen and their offspring were allowed butter, while courtiers had to make do with dripping. 'Common folk' were permitted three courses: on meat days, cabbage or peas, a piece of dried cow meat, and porridge; on fish days, herring, dried fish, and porridge and butter.

In the affluent homes of the late Middle Ages, the family sat along one side of the table to facilitate service. There were no plates or cutlery. People would cut large slices of bread and eat their meat or fish off them, rather like the Romans used trenchers.

Afterwards, honey or fruit juice would be poured over the bread to turn it into a dessert, or it would be given to the poor along with other scraps. It was considered bad manners to lick your fingers clean or to dry them on your sleeves, so Danes would wipe them on the table cloth.

Plates first appeared at court around 1500 and, as with so many of the Danish culinary customs, the middle classes and the aristocracy were quick to follow the royal lead. Only the rich, however, owned cutlery for guests, so people had to bring their own. As in so many countries, much of the food was then eaten off a common dish in the centre of the table.

The first cookery book printed in Danish dates from 1616, and was probably translated from the German. Earlier recipes have been found, however, in handwritten papers ascribed to Henrik Harpestreng, a doctor and priest who died in 1244. These reflect the French, German and English cookery of the time, and make use of spices which were then much too expensive for any but the very rich to use. By the sixteenth century, however, Denmark had become one of the world's great naval powers and had no difficulty in getting spices from the Far East. They became cheaper, and cooks ran riot in their use. It is uncertain when a reaction to this began to set in, but set in it did and the characteristic Danish cuisine today, like that of other northern countries, is bland compared with, for example, Mediterranean cooking.

In 1646 Arent Berntsen's *Denmark's and Norway's Bountiful Splendour* appeared. This told householders, be they courtiers, warriors, sailors or workers, how to plan their short-term and long-term purchases. It was extremely important to the families of old to make certain that there were ample stores available for any length of time, and household accounts were kept very carefully. The measure used by Berntsen was 'courses', each 'course' sufficing for eight people. For example, one sheep's carcase would yield $3\frac{1}{2}$ courses; 1 fresh oxen, 40 courses; 1 barrel of pigs' trotters, 60 courses; 1 barrel of tripe with no feet added, 70 courses; 1 barrel of herring, 100 courses; and 1 turkey cock, 1 course.

When converted into modern decimal measures, the

men of a naval station at that time were given, every day, 600 grammes of bread and four pots of beer. On each of the three meat days, a further 330g pork, 610g beef, 175g peas, and on fish days 225g cod, 130g dried fish, 100g butter and 130g hulled grain. It was still common to have three courses for every meal, but the rich had many, many more.

The court still led the way in eating habits, but the quality of the food did not always impress foreign guests. British visitor Robert Sidney stayed at the court of the colourful architect-king Christian IV in 1632, and afterwards wrote: 'The fare was the worst I have ever encountered and we sat at the table for a very long time. The King himself cut for me off every dish. There were two rounds, each consisting of ten courses, plus twelve puddings.'

In 1703 there appeared a cookery book which contained many authentic Danish recipes. It showed some French influence, but on the whole the recipes had become simpler, and employed fewer spices. The growing importance of porridge and soup was reflected, but the most striking feature was the use of more fresh products rather than those which had been dried, salted or smoked.

During the second half of the eighteenth century there was growing talk of the need for greater restraint in living standards, and many thought that the balance of trade could be improved, 'not to speak of the need for greater earnestness and improved customs and morals'. In 1772, a law popularly called the 'Luxury Bill' introduced many restrictions in Denmark and Norway, then both under the Danish crown. No one was allowed to serve more than eight courses for dinner, though this severity was tempered by the addition: 'apart from salads, plus no more than four kinds of puddings and foreign fruits'. Festive evening meals could not exceed six dishes plus two puddings; two dishes and two puddings extra were permitted for weddings. Farmers were admonished for their 'deplorable opulence' and told to invite no more than thirty-two people to weddings, to serve four courses only and no coffee or wine.

It was in this century that the potato arrived in Denmark, probably with the Huguenots in 1719. But potatoes came into their own in the 1760s when the first efforts were made to cultivate the vast moorland areas in Jutland. They were to assume immense importance in the Danish diet.

However important the influence of the upper classes or the well-off townspeople, the farming population at this time accounted for perhaps ninety per cent of the population, and it was their style of living which increasingly set the rhythm of everyday life, and the composition of so many Danish dishes. Therefore, even though more fresh ingredients were used, food was still prepared for days in advance. Wife and maids had to work hard making porridges, stews and soups with meats, vegetables, dumplings and always making good use of left-overs. Small wonder that this has left its imprint on the present-day style of Danish cooking. Soups with vegetables, small meat balls and tiny dumplings are reminiscent of the days when the meat balls would have been much bigger and the dumplings very much more substantial. Yellow pea soup and kale soup are still served with boiled meat on a separate plate. Meat and poultry are still pot roasted, and the stock turned into gravy to utilize every bit of the delicious juices.

Long before the advent of the streamlined Danish Landrace pig and super-hygienic bacon factories, the pig played an important role in kitchen economy. The entire household, as well as the local slaughterer, would help turn the vast hogs of those days into dozens and dozens of delicacies, and no sooner was everything done than a party was given for friends and neighbours. Slaughter time, normally around November, was therefore one round of parties, all with numerous hot and cold dishes. In the town, too, a pattern of entertaining evolved with housewives set on showing their culinary skills in as many ways as possible. By the mid-nineteenth century, entertaining had become an art in Denmark.

In 1837, a Madam Mangor wrote the first truly Danish cookbook aimed at the average household. It is still Denmark's best-known book in the field. In it, she listed what she thought to be the three most important requirements for a pleasant meal: definite and firm meal times; a snow-white table cloth and a tidily laid table; and the housewife's kind and smiling face. This applied equally to simple family meals and more lavish occasions when a household was entertaining.

An evening at the home of friends in Copenhagen in 1840 would be a long and leisurely one, not so different to the pattern in Britain at that time. The guests would arrive around 6.00 in the evening and be seated around the tea table in front of the sofa. At the hostess's place stood the tea machine, and on the table baskets full of sweet rusks, cinnamon fingers, and buttered wheat rusks. After tea, the men played cards and the women knitted. It was a welcome interruption when the big tray was put on the table with bowls of cherry marmalade, redcurrant jelly and raspberry jam, and in the middle a cut glass full of water and teaspoons. The guests would then take a spoon, taste the various delicacies, and put the spoon back in the water for someone else to use. The men were given rum or brandy with a slice of ox tongue, salami or Gruyère cheese.

At 9.00 the party went to the dinner table for a proper meal often consisting of a couple of hot dishes, such as salmon and a good joint, and rounded off with a splendid cake. Sometimes, however, a Cold Table was served instead. A few glass plates with slices of cold meat did not suffice: 'The guests would arrive armed with good appetite and preferred to see for themselves what they were given to eat. Therefore everything had to be put on the table uncut, and on such occasions the table flowed over with food. At one end the whole roast goose, at the other end the whole smoked ham with neatly folded paper around the shank. In between these proud flank-men was now placed the remainder of the forces, consisting of an ox tongue, a large piece of smoked salmon, rolled, spiced pork, salted beef, salami, egg, anchovies, cheese, etc.' (from Gyldendal's *Blå Kogebog*). The Danish Cold Table described later in this book had emerged.

But times were changing. The war with Prussia in 1864 cost Denmark the province of Schleswig-Holstein and caused much bitterness, but it engendered a new national spirit and a thirst for learning and development. Young girls of farm stock and of the middle classes, instead of learning at home or working for others, were now taught good housekeeping in a host of domestic science schools or in Folk High Schools, and nutrition and good planning helped in developing the Danish diet. At the same time, Danish agriculture found new strength and new markets, first of all in newly industrialized and hungry Britain. For the first time, Danish farmers had to consider the requirements of their customers overseas and did so by a unique system of co-operation which set up uniform standards of high quality for their products. For seventy years the Danish State Quality Control, set up at the request

of the farmers themselves, has contributed to the high standards of hygiene and quality of Danish bacon, butter, cheese and canned meats.

Modern times have seen the development of the affluent society in the western world demanding unparalleled standards of quality and freshness in food, demands which the Danish food producers have been both eager and able to meet. Today they deliver quality foodstuffs to Britain and markets throughout the world in a state of freshness that has never before been equalled in exports of such great volume.

Manufacturing and design skills have brought Denmark into the late twentieth century as an industrial nation but it is the farmers' dedication to quality food production which will give Denmark, a small country of just over five million people, a place in history as food purveyors extraordinary to the world. These egalitarian people, few of whom have too much and fewer still too little, offer a practical example of the benefits of a voluntary co-operative agricultural and food processing system. It is not without its problems but it has an inherent strength that their early Viking ancestors would recognize and salute today.

Table Customs in Denmark Today

Though their eating habits have an element of sobriety, the Danes are second to none in making a festive table the highlight of any celebration, and few countries have thought of more excuses for celebrations and of more variations in the fare to suit those occasions. France is, of course, the cradle of intricate and splendidly ornamental *haute cuisine*, but Denmark is the place where, today, an ambitious cook will find most inspiration for the presentation of meals.

Everyday eating habits have the needs of centuries of hard work by farmers and craftsmen behind them. The day starts early, in towns as well as the country, and lunch hours are short – Danes like to get home early, eat an early meal and have a long evening in front of them.

In the early morning breakfast, more likely than not, is coffee and a fresh roll from the baker – with cool butter, a slice of cheese or a little jam, and perhaps a boiled egg. Bacon is virtually unknown at that hour of the day. One-third of all households still eat porridge for breakfast.

In the course of the morning, there is a quick coffee

break and later, around 12 noon, comes lunch, usually a packet of *smørrebrød* (open sandwiches) with an apple or a tomato. Even if the office or factory has a canteen, or people dash out to a nearby cafeteria, the 'flat' style of *smørrebrød* is the staple food and a glass of milk or a cup of coffee the beverage.

Another quick coffee break is taken in the afternoon, perhaps with a piece of pastry, and then work ends at 4.00 or 5.00. With not all that far to travel home, dinner at 6.00 is no problem. The evening meal is at most two courses. With the late cup of coffee, around 9.30 or 10.00, there might be a snack – cake, pastry or a cheese *smørrebrød*.

British tourists in Denmark look in vain for pubs, but the social life lies within the home and does not make a pub a home away from home. There is solace in the licensing hours though, and you can have a drink at just about any time. Lager beer is the national drink. Pilsner is the commonest type. It is the drink to have with food. Wine and spirits are reserved for special festive celebrations.

With your lunchtime beer you will, on festive occasions at least, have *snaps*, water-clear potato- or barley-based alcohol, mostly with caraway flavour but occasionally flavoured with other herbs. It is served ice-cold – sometimes the bottle is encased in a block of ice to achieve this – and not sipped. *Snaps* is hardly ever drunk with warm food but is ideal with sharp, marinated herrings and with cheese. The Danes are rightly proud of their *snaps*, which should not be confused with the German word *schnapps*. Supermarkets are well stocked with imported wines, there being no home-grown wine from grapes as Denmark lies too far north for that. On formal occasions the French custom is adopted of serving white wine with the fish followed by a red wine with the meat course, and very often a glass of sweet wine, madeira or port with the sweet course.

There is no real 'cocktail hour' because dinner is taken so early in the evening; any social drinking tends to take place after the meal. That is the time for another beer, a glass of wine, or a liqueur.

Coffee is an important beverage in Denmark and no grocer will enjoy good business unless his coffee is freshly roasted and popular with his customers – rather the way bacon is the hallmark of a good British grocer. The Danish colloquialism for strong coffee is 'midwife's coffee'. Even today, many expectant mothers prefer to have their babies at home, and while it is well-known that the first requirement when preparing for a delivery is plenty of boiling hot water, in Denmark you add strong coffee and cigars for the

midwife. The Danish equivalent to Irish coffee is to put a small silver coin in an empty cup, pour in strong black coffee until the coin is no longer visible, and then add *snaps* until it shows again! Cream should not be added to this brew.

Though it is nearly a century and a half since Madam Mangor stipulated the three most important requirements for a pleasant meal, her words still express all that is best in the Danish attitude to food. Throughout Denmark, a good meal is treated with respect; good food is made to be served at a given time, and should not be kept waiting. Much more colour is used today than in the nineteenth century – in the table cloth, food, and decorations – but much emphasis is still placed on a neatly laid table. And Madame Mangor's last sentiment – 'the housewife's kind and smiling face' – is reflected in other customs, notably the striking feature of Danish foodmanship: the second helping. If you are a guest in someone's home, you will almost always be offered a second helping, at least of the main dish. When done with 'a smiling face', it is a very endearing habit.

Meals are for being together and not just for filling up, say the Danes. So when celebrating, a number of acknowledgements by hosts and fellow guests are happily observed.

On arrival, guests express their gratitude for being invited, and the host reciprocates by thanking the guests for coming. On meeting other guests, you should shake hands or you may be considered reserved.

No one drinks at the table before the host has said his *Velkommen* (welcome) followed by the first *skål*. This famous invitation to drink is undoubtedly the only Danish word known all over the world. Whoever issues the invitation begins by drawing the attention of one other person, or indeed the whole table. With raised glass, he looks into the eyes of one or all, nods solemnly and says '*skål*', and lifts his glass a little.

Everyone reciprocates the gesture and toasts, as much in unison as possible, trying to coincide the moment when the glasses are again at nose-level. There follows another, perhaps less solemn nod, and only then are the glasses put down.

Traditionally a *snaps* should be drained with each *skål* but this custom is no longer always observed. You *may* sip from your glass in between, but you do miss out on something if you do not add to your evening the pleasure of sending a friendly message to someone in this way. At smaller dinner parties, 'skåling' aloud is mostly left to the host or hostess – lest the guest be assumed overly thirsty. But this does not prevent a silent version from taking place between individuals.

At the end of the meal, the host says 'Velbekomme' – which means 'I hope you liked it', and you reply with 'Tak for mad' – thanks for the meal. Do not be surprised if, in Danish company, some or all guests follow up with a handshake.

The bread-and-butter letter is virtually unknown in Denmark, but it is just as important when you meet your hosts again to remember to say 'Tak for sidst' – thank you for the time we were last together.

When it comes to entertaining it is the warm feeling that comes from the heart, not the date on the calendar, that makes the occasion in Denmark. The refreshments can be just a cup of coffee and a biscuit but the lighted candles on the table in the evening make guests welcome in a special way. For Danish people the home is the centre around which they do their entertaining. Unexpected guests are as welcome as invited ones and consequently meals have developed a rather elastic style which can be confusing to the stranger. These meals have the great advantage of making the food go round, within an established and really quite formal pattern, even if there is not a lot of one particular item. A meal of *smørrebrød* may be filled out with the addition of a quickly prepared small hot dish such as bacon and egg cake. If there is not time to prepare *smørrebrød*, then the food is put out in attractive small dishes and everyone makes his own. The small hot dish then follows. A more elaborate meal yet still without the formal pattern of three or more courses is the Cold Table (pages 97–100). It is a pity that no one has found a truly descriptive name in English for this Danish food tradition.

Imaginative table settings are as important as the menu in Danish homes. Naturally these are based on the very attractive Danish china, table linen and tableware which may not be available elsewhere, but it is quite easy to follow the custom of working out a colour scheme for each occasion. Many families in Britain do this already at Christmas and Easter time but there's a lot to be said for it all the year round.

Danish families love to orchestrate their table settings to reflect the colours of the season. For example, in the spring they might choose a yellow table cloth, napkins and candles, with blue, white, or green china – many colours look well on plain yellow. When flowers are expensive, candles in small bowls with flowers arranged around the base are used. In the summer, flower petals are often scattered informally on the cloth, or the table may be decorated with wild flowers – buttercups, meadowsweet and wild mint – or summer grasses. Autumn calls for browns and oranges, with beech leaves, dried flowers, late fresh blooms of marigolds or chrysanthemums or even dried ornamental gourds. In the dark days of winter, little pots of snowdrops or crocuses can be bought at florists' shops once Christmas decorations have been put away.

Soups and Starters

The mixture of traditional and modern recipes in this chapter shows clearly how cooking has changed not only in Denmark but wherever people like to cook with a Danish flavour.

Soups, though still important today, were even more so in olden times when most people worked on the land. Hearty and warming, the traditional Danish soups were often substantial enough to be a main dish, with their additions of vegetables, meats and dumplings. In winter Danes enjoy *Gule ærter med flæsk*, a yellow pea soup cooked with lightly salted or fresh pork and sausages. This is a main course, the meat and any potatoes being served separately while the broth from the meat is added to the peas. Clear soup too is very popular. The meat or flour dumplings often served with it today are tiny in size, but no doubt were more substantial years ago. These dumplings are rather time-consuming to make and, like the soups to which they are added, are not always home-made. Danish cooks put tinned and packet soups and stock cubes to good use like cooks elsewhere, though still agreeing that there is nothing quite so pleasant as the home-made kind when time permits.

Old-fashioned soups made with various fruits gave variety to winters long ago. Although now rarely served to start a meal, fruit soup is still sometimes made for dessert.

A bunch of pot herbs known as the *suppevisk*, comprising the green tops of leeks, celery leaves and some parsley, is used for flavouring. These are tied together and lowered into the pot and may be used with or without the addition of a bouquet garni. They indicate the thriftiness of Danish cooking where nothing that may be used is thrown away.

The starter is much in vogue in Denmark today but it is rather a new idea and is one of those fashion changes that occur in food from time to time. Town-dwellers in particular, with their different lifestyle, often prefer to begin a meal with a light dish to whet the appetite rather than soup. Instructions for serving the marinated or salt herrings which frequently start a Danish meal will be found in the chapter on fish. Selected Danish open sandwiches (pages 85–95) make an attractive first course, too.

Green Kale Soup
Grønkålssuppe

500g (1lb) salted pork	*250g (8oz) curly kale*
(shoulder or similar)	*2 leeks*
250g (8oz) potatoes	*salt and pepper*
250g (8oz) carrots	*350g (12oz) pork sausages*
1.8 litres (3 pints) water	

Boil the piece of salted pork with the whole, peeled potatoes and carrots in the water. Cook until tender, about 1½ hours. Take out the pork and keep it hot.

Remove coarse stalks from the kale and wash well. Trim and wash the leeks. Put kale and leeks through a mincer, or chop them finely. Add the prepared kale and leeks to the stock and stir well, breaking up the potatoes and carrots. Simmer for a further 20 minutes. Season the soup to taste with pepper and a little salt.

Boil the sausages separately and serve with the meat as for yellow pea soup (page 16). *Serves 4–6.*

Green Kale Soup

Old-fashioned Cabbage Soup Gammeldags kålsuppe

500g (1lb) lightly salted pork	750g (1½lb) cabbage
1.5 litres (2½ pints) water	2 carrots
4 peppercorns	2 sticks celery
1 suppevisk (green tops of leeks and celery with parsley tied with cotton)	1 leek
	250g (8oz) potatoes
	salt and pepper

Bring the meat to the boil in the water and skim carefully. Add the peppercorns and *suppevisk*, and boil gently for about 1 hour. Wash the cabbage, discard outer leaves and cut remainder coarsely. Scrape and chop the carrots. Wash and chop celery and leek. Peel and dice the potatoes. Add the prepared vegetables to the soup and cook for a further ½ hour. Lift out the meat on to a separate serving dish. Discard the *suppevisk*. Taste the soup and season with pepper and salt if required. Bring the soup to the table in a tureen and serve with slices of the cooked meat and French mustard, as a main course. *Serves 4–6.*

Cauliflower and Cheese Soup Blomkål- og ostesuppe

50g (2oz) Danish Blue cheese	1 litre (1¾ pints) chicken stock
1 medium-sized cauliflower	40g (1½oz) butter
250g (8oz) onions, chopped	25g (1oz) plain flour
	pepper

Grate the Danish Blue cheese using the coarse side of the grater. Wash the cauliflower and trim off the bigger outside leaves. Cut the cauliflower into sprigs and place them in a large saucepan with the chopped onion and chicken stock. Cover and cook slowly for 10–15 minutes until the cauliflower is just tender. Purée cauliflower and stock using a sieve or liquidizer.

Gently melt the butter in a large saucepan. Stir in the flour and cook for 1 minute. Gradually add the cauliflower purée, stirring all the time. Bring to the boil and cook gently for 3 minutes. Add the grated Danish Blue cheese, a little at a time, and stir until dissolved. Taste and adjust seasoning. Serve with butter-fried *croûtons* and chopped parsley.

To make *croûtons* follow instructions in the recipe for Cold Buttermilk Soup (page 20), omitting the sugar. *Serves 4–6.*

Yellow Pea Soup with Pork Gule ærter med flæsk

This famous dish of yellow peas, cooked meat and sausages is a great favourite with Danish men. If the soup is not thick enough for their liking when it comes to table, some people stir a little mild-flavoured vinegar into their plates, which instantly thickens it. Use wine vinegar if you want to try this, as strong malt vinegar will spoil the taste.

Pancakes are served afterwards to complete the meal, the peas and meat being the main course. This soup is one of the few main dishes with which *snaps* is served.

The quantities given here will serve eight and it is customary to serve it on two consecutive days. The soup is reheated the next day but the meat and sausage are served cold. If you want to make a small quantity, reduce the peas and their cooking water by half and use only 500g (1lb) of meat with enough water to cover it and 250g (½lb) sausages. The same quantities of vegetables can be used.

500g (1lb) yellow split peas	parsley
	thyme
2 litres (3½ pints) water	1kg (2lb) lightly salted or fresh streaky pork
2–3 carrots	
2 sticks celery	1 litre (1¾ pints) water
1 parsnip	500g (1lb) pork sausages
2 medium-sized leeks	salt and pepper
250g (8oz) small onions	

Rinse the peas and put them to soak overnight in 2 litres (3½ pints) cold water. Next day, bring them to the boil in the soaking water, skim, and simmer for about 1½ hours without the lid until the water is absorbed and thickened by the peas.

Prepare the vegetables. Keep the leek tops and celery leaves, wash them and tie them into a bunch

Old-fashioned Cabbage Soup

Cauliflower and Cheese Soup

Yellow Pea Soup with Pork

with the parsley and thyme to make a *suppevisk*. Put the meat in a saucepan with the 1 litre (1¾ pints) water, add the vegetables, except peas, and the *suppevisk*. Simmer until the meat is tender, about 2 hours.

Boil the sausages in a separate pan for 10–15 minutes and keep them hot.

When the pork is tender take it out of the cooking water and put it with the sausages. Discard the *suppevisk*. Add the cooked sliced vegetables and some of the meat stock to the peas to produce a fairly thick soup. Taste the soup and add salt if required, and pepper.

The soup is served in soup plates with slices of the meat and sausages on a side plate. Good accompaniments are boiled potatoes, rye bread and French mustard. *Serves 8.*

Bacon and Bean Soup

Bacon- og bønnesuppe

1 gammon knuckle or slipper, about 500g (1lb)
250g (8oz) haricot or black-eyed beans
2 sticks celery
3 carrots
2 onions
1 litre (1¾ pints) water
bouquet garni
300ml (½ pint) milk or milk and single cream
chopped parsley
pepper

Separately soak the gammon knuckle and beans overnight in cold water. Next day, drain the beans and remove the gammon knuckle from the water. Strip the rind from the knuckle.

Prepare and chop the vegetables and place them in a large pan with the water, stripped knuckle and bouquet garni. Simmer for ½ hour, add soaked beans and simmer for a further 1–1½ hours until the gammon is tender. Remove the knuckle from the pan, dice the meat into cubes and return to the soup. Add the milk, or milk and cream, plenty of chopped parsley and reheat gently. Season with pepper before serving.

Serve as a main course with French bread and butter. *Serves 4–6*

Quick Garden Soup

Nem grønsagssuppe

250g (8oz) leeks
2 medium-sized onions
50g (2oz) butter
1 litre (1¾ pints) stock
½ litre (¾ pint) milk
pinch dried thyme
250g (8oz) peas or diced carrots (frozen)
150ml (¼ pint) whipping cream
salt and pepper
chives or green tops of spring onions
50g (2oz) grated Danish Cheddar cheese

Finely chop the leeks and onions, and fry them without browning in the butter for 5 minutes. Add the stock, milk and thyme, and cook for 10 minutes. Add the diced carrots or peas and cook a further 5 minutes. Stir in cream and check seasoning. Serve immediately with chopped chives or spring onion on top, and pass grated cheese separately.

If fresh peas and carrots are used, the soup should be simmered a further 15 minutes before cream is added. *Serves 4–6.*

Chicken Broth with Dumplings

Hønsekødsuppe med kødboller

This is an unusual recipe because two meals are prepared at once. The chicken used for the broth, customarily a boiling fowl, is served later in a horseradish sauce as a main dish (page 44), or you may prefer to have the chicken first and serve the broth later.

1.35-kg (3-lb) chicken
3 litres (5 pints) water
250g (8oz) carrots
2 leeks
1 stick celery
good bunch parsley
bouquet garni
salt
meat and flour balls (see page 19)

Clean the chicken and bring to the boil in the water. Remove any scum which may form. Add the prepared vegetables, and the parsley and bouquet garni. Season with a little salt. The vegetables may be removed when cooked or left in the broth. Cover and simmer the

18

chicken for 1 hour or longer until it is tender.

When the chicken is cooked remove it from the broth and set aside to serve as a main course (page 44).

Remove bouquet garni, taste and adjust seasoning. Add sufficient gravy browning to obtain a good colour, if liked. Heat the meat balls and flour balls through in the soup before serving. *Serves 10.*

Meat Balls for Soup
Kødboller til suppe

250g (8oz) minced pork	45ml (3 tbsp) flour
½ onion	300ml (½ pint) milk or
5ml (1 tsp) salt	stock
pinch pepper	white of 1 egg

Put the meat through the mincer again 2 or 3 times with the onion until really fine. Add salt and pepper. Stir the flour to a paste with most of the milk or stock and stir into the meat a little at a time together with the lightly beaten egg white. It is an advantage to mix the meat well and let it rest from time to time while mixing. It can then absorb more liquid and becomes lighter and more spongy. Form into small balls with a teaspoon and drop into boiling water to which a little salt has been added. Boil for 4–5 minutes, until cooked. Lift out with a perforated spoon, place in a sieve, rinse with cold water, and let them drip until dry. Usually these meat balls are made the day before, and then warmed up in the soup when needed. Add to clear soup or tomato soup. *Makes 30–40.*

Flour Balls for Soup
Melboller til suppe

75g (3oz) butter	3 eggs
200ml (7fl oz) water	5ml (1 tsp) salt
125g (4½oz) flour	

Bring the butter and water to the boil and meanwhile sieve the flour. Remove from the heat, stir in the sieved flour all at once and, when smooth and shiny, replace over the heat and cook until the paste leaves the side of the pan and forms a ball. Cool the paste and mix in the eggs, one at a time, beating well. The paste should be stiff enough to stand in peaks. Add salt.

Bring a pan of water to the boil, adding 5ml (1 tsp) salt per 1 litre (1¾ pints) water. Reduce heat and add the paste in heaped teaspoonfuls to the water. The water must not boil at the moment the balls are being put in. Bring quickly to the boil and, as soon as they boil, add a little cold water. Bring back to the boil and again add a little cold water. After repeating this three times, the balls will be cooked and feel firm. Lift out with a perforated spoon and drain in a sieve. If the flour balls are allowed to boil for any length of time they will become loose and crumble. Add to clear soup, celery soup etc. *Makes 30.*

Mussel Soup
Muslingesuppe

25g (1oz) butter	50g (2 oz) plain flour
1 onion	50g (2oz) butter, softened
150-g (5¼-oz) tin mussels in own juice	15ml (1 tbsp) chopped parsley
300ml (½ pint) water	150ml (¼ pint) single
300ml (½ pint) dry white wine	cream
	salt and pepper

Melt the butter in a saucepan, add the chopped onion and cook for 1 minute. Add the mussels, water and white wine, and allow to boil for 5 minutes. Work the flour into the softened butter to form a paste. Add this paste, a little at a time, to the soup, whisking continuously until the soup thickens. Add chopped parsley, then finally stir in the cream and add seasoning. Serve with warm poppy seed rolls (page 105). *Serves 4.*

Fruit Soup
Frugtsuppe

With the richer diet of modern times fruit soups are out of favour with townsfolk to start a meal, but are occasionally served as dessert. In the countryside, however, people still gather all kinds of berries and fruits from hedgerow and garden to turn into soups. Elderberries, blackberries, redcurrants, black-currants, raspberries, gooseberries, apples and pears are all used. Elderberry is considered a good remedy for coughs and colds.

Soft fruit is washed and put in a pan with enough water to cover, cooked until soft and then strained through a jelly bag or sieved. Sugar is added roughly in the proportions of 500g (1lb) to each litre ($1\frac{3}{4}$ pints) juice, the whole brought to the boil until the sugar dissolves. The syrup is then diluted and thickened to make the soup or bottled for use later.

Rosehip syrup is not always made in advance. Sometimes the hips are threaded on to string and hung from the ceiling to dry. When needed they are boiled, sieved off and used as required.

Pear soup is flavoured with cinnamon and thickened with split barley. Cinnamon and lemon go well with apple, and so do cloves as in the recipe here.

These thin soups are thickened with potato flour, rice, sago or semolina and sultanas are often added. They have the consistency of a thick pea soup when served.

This apple soup (*æblesuppe*) can be served before or after the main course.

750g ($1\frac{1}{2}$lb) cooking apples 25g (1oz) arrowroot or
3–4 cloves   potato flour
1 litre ($1\frac{3}{4}$ pints) water   sugar

Wash and peel the apples. Place the peel and cloves in the water and simmer for 30 minutes. Meanwhile keep the apples covered in cold water with a dash of lemon added to prevent browning.

Strain the peel. Slice the apples into the juice and cook apples until soft. Mix the arrowroot or potato flour with a little cold water and add to the apples with sugar to taste to sweeten slightly. Simmer for a few minutes to thicken slightly. Do not boil if potato flour is used. The soup may be sieved or served with the apples in pieces. Serve warm as soup with butter-fried *croûtons* (see cold buttermilk soup) or cold as a dessert with sponge fingers. *Serves 5.*

Yoghurt Soup
Yoghurtsuppe

This is a perfect soup to serve cold on a summer's day, especially if you can substitute fresh herbs from the garden.

$\frac{1}{4}$ cucumber   5ml (1 tsp) dried dill
15 radishes   2.5ml ($\frac{1}{2}$ tsp) dried
600ml (1 pint) yoghurt   tarragon
300ml ($\frac{1}{2}$ pint) milk   pinch dried mint
30ml (2 tbsp) chopped   10ml (2 tsp) salt
   chives or green tops of   2.5ml ($\frac{1}{2}$ tsp) white pepper
   spring onions

Cut the cucumber into small dice and slice the radishes. Mix yoghurt and milk, add remaining ingredients and the prepared cucumber and radishes. Mix well. Thin with extra milk if the soup is too thick. Serve very cold. *Serves 5–6.*

Cold Buttermilk Soup
Kærnemælkskoldskål

Light and cooling to serve in the summertime, this is more of a drink than a soup. Commercially prepared buttermilk may need thinning with a little fresh milk.

2 eggs   Croûtons:
40g ($1\frac{1}{2}$oz) sugar   2 slices white bread
910ml (32fl oz) buttermilk   25g (1oz) sugar (optional)
   (2 cartons)   50g (2oz) butter
peel of 1 large lemon

Whisk the eggs well with the sugar. Add the buttermilk and grated lemon peel and mix thoroughly. To make the *croûtons* cut the bread into small even squares and mix with the sugar, if used. Melt the butter in a frying pan and fry the bread until golden brown. Let the *croûtons* cool in the frying pan after cooking, then serve with the soup. *Serves 4–6.*

Hot Buttermilk Soup

Varm kærnemælkssuppe

25g (1oz) sultanas
15g (½oz) butter
15g (½oz) plain flour
455ml (16fl oz) buttermilk (1 carton)
5ml (1 tsp) granulated sugar

Put the sultanas to soak in a little warm water. Make a white sauce by melting the butter, stirring in the flour and cooking it for 1–2 minutes without letting it colour. Gradually add the buttermilk, stirring all the time over a gentle heat until smooth and creamy. Add the sugar and stir to dissolve. Drain the sultanas and add them to the soup. Heat through and serve. *Serves 2–3.*

Danish Cheese Mousse and *Tarteletter*

Danish Cheese Mousse

Dansk ostemousse

100g (4oz) Danish Blue cheese
100g (4oz) Samsoe cheese
300ml (½ pint) double cream
25g (1oz) chopped walnuts
30ml (2 tbsp) water
15g (½oz) aspic jelly powder
2 egg whites
pepper
5ml (1 tsp) made mustard and/or 5ml (1 tsp) celery salt
maraschino cherries and parsley to garnish

Finely grate both cheeses into a large bowl. Partially whip the cream and add with the walnuts to the cheese. Add the water to the aspic powder in a small bowl and stand it in a pan of hot water until dissolved. Allow to cool. Whisk the egg whites stiffly and fold them into the cheese mixture, then season with pepper, mustard and celery salt. Fold in aspic. Pour the mixture into a 500-g (1-lb) loaf tin or other suitable 600-ml (1-pint) container and put in a cool place to set.

When required turn out the mousse and decorate it with maraschino cherries and parsley sprigs. Serve as a starter or a savoury with melba toast and butter. *Serves 6–8.*

Tarteletter

Tarteletter

These crisp and elegant pastry cases are used to hold savoury fillings and are served as a starter to a meal. Allow one or two for each person. In Denmark the pastry cases can be bought ready-made, and filled as needed (see overleaf).

150g (5oz) chilled butter
250g (9oz) plain flour
2.5ml (½ tsp) salt
1 egg
10ml (2 tsp) single cream

Set the oven at 220°C (425°F)/Gas 7.

Cut the butter into the flour and salt and lightly rub it in with your fingertips until the mixture resembles breadcrumbs. For ease the butter should be well chilled and firm before use. Add the beaten egg and cream to form a dough. Knead lightly. Cover the dough in cling wrap and stand it in a cold place for 1 hour. The dough is best handled cold and is easiest to work when used half at a time. If it becomes warm it will stick to the rolling pin and require additional flour which results in a less crisp pastry.

Roll out the dough thinly. Cut out 10-cm (4-in) rounds and carefully line some greased tartlet cases. Use a small piece of dough to press the pastry into shape. Place the lined tins in the refrigerator for at least ½ hour before baking. Prick the dough lightly and bake for 8–10 minutes until golden brown. *Makes 20–24 cases.*

21

Savoury Fillings for Tarteletter

Fyld til tarteletter

FISH BALLS IN SHRIMP SAUCE

15g (½oz) butter
15g (½oz) flour
275-g (10-oz) can fish balls

50g (2oz) shrimps
salt and pepper
anchovy essence

Melt the butter and stir in the flour. Add the juice from the fish balls little by little to make a smooth sauce. Fold in the fish balls and the shrimps. Season sauce and colour slightly with anchovy essence. *Fills 10–12 tarteletter cases.*

CHICKEN AND MUSHROOM

15g (½oz) butter
15g (½oz) flour
200ml (7fl oz) milk
100g (4oz) mushrooms, cooked and sliced

225g (8oz) cooked chicken
salt and pepper
15ml (1 tbsp) sherry
parsley

To make the sauce, melt the butter and stir in the flour. Add the milk little by little, stirring well. Cook 2–3 minutes. Add the mushrooms and the chopped chicken. Season and add the sherry. Fill the *tarteletter* cases and sprinkle with chopped parsley. *Fills 10–12 tarteletter cases.*

CHOPPED HAM IN CREAMED SPINACH

15g (½oz) butter
15g (½oz) flour
200ml (7fl oz) milk

175g (6oz) cooked ham, cut in cubes
1 small packet of frozen spinach, thawed

Make a white sauce as above, and add the ham and the spinach. Reserve a few cubes of ham for garnish. Heat through, pour into 10–12 *tarteletter* and top with remaining ham.

VEGETABLES IN CHEESE WITH CRISPY BACON

15g (½oz) butter
15g (½oz) flour
200ml (7fl oz) milk
226-g (8-oz) packet of frozen mixed vegetables

50g (2oz) Samsoe cheese, grated
salt and pepper
6–8 rashers bacon

Make a white sauce as above. Add the cooked vegetables and the cheese, then season. Fill 10–12 *tarteletter*, and decorate with pieces of crispy bacon.

Grapefruit Mould with Crab Salad
Grapefrugtrand med krabbesalat

500-g (1-lb) can grapefruit segments
20g (¾oz) powdered gelatine or 6 leaves
600ml (1 pint) white wine and grapefruit juice

50ml (2fl oz) double cream
200g (7oz) mayonnaise
200g (7oz) crab or other shellfish
½ 275-g (10-oz) can asparagus

Strain the grapefruit and add the gelatine to the juice. Soak for five minutes and then heat very gently until dissolved. Add the white wine to make the grapefruit juice up to 600ml (1 pint). When the jelly is beginning to thicken, pour a little into the bottom of a 1½-litre (2½-pint) ring mould. Arrange the grapefruit segments on top, and then add the rest of the jelly. Leave in a cool place until set.

Fold the double cream into the mayonnaise, then add the crab meat and the drained asparagus cut into lengths.

Turn the mould out on to a plate and pile the crab salad into the centre. *Serves 7–8.*

Karen's Fish Dish
Karens Fiskeret

8 fillets plaice
pinch salt
45ml (3 tbsp) dry white wine or lemon juice

100g (4oz) butter
4 egg yolks
1 tomato
6 olives

Roll the fish and place them in an ovenproof dish. Season with salt and add white wine or lemon juice and 25g (1oz) butter. Cover the dish and put it in the oven at 200°C (400°F)/Gas 6 for 15 minutes. Strain the stock, and keep the fish hot.

Mix the stock with 75g (3oz) melted butter and the well-beaten egg yolks. Heat the mixture in a double saucepan, stirring constantly, until the sauce begins to thicken. Pour the sauce over the fish, garnish with slices of tomato and olives, and serve hot. *Serves 4.*

Tomatoes with Danish Blue

Tomater med Danablu

Serve this on shredded lettuce leaves, to start a meal or as part of a Cold Table.

4 large firm tomatoes	50g (2oz) Danish Blue
1 eating apple	cheese
8 stuffed green olives	60ml (4 tbsp) mayonnaise
1 stalk celery	little chopped parsley

Cut the tops off the tomatoes and scoop out the flesh. Place the tomatoes upside down to drain the juice. Peel, core and chop apple, slice olives finely, slice the celery stalk and cut the Danish Blue cheese into small cubes. Mix the mayonnaise with the sieved flesh of the tomatoes. Fill the tomatoes with the prepared ingredients and pour the mayonnaise over. Decorate with chopped parsley. *Serves 4.*

Mussels with Bacon

Muslinger med bacon

10–12 rashers streaky	20–24 mussels, freshly
bacon	cooked or canned

Stretch the bacon rashers slightly, using the back of a knife, and cut them in half. Wrap half a rasher round each mussel and secure with a cocktail stick. Fry or grill until crisp. Serve hot as tit-bits with drinks or as a first course with spinach in sauce (page 67). *Serves 4–5 as a starter.*

Consommé Cheese Starter

Consommé og oste hors-d'œuvre

425-g (15-oz) can clear	double cream
consommé	50-g (2-oz) jar lumpfish
75g (3oz) Danish Blue	roe 'caviar'
cheese	lemon and parsley to
little curry powder	garnish
pepper	

Chill the consommé for several hours.

Crumble the cheese into a liquidizer, add the consommé and blend them together. Stir in a pinch of curry powder and a little pepper. Pour into individual soufflé dishes and leave in a cool place until set. Top each with a little whipped cream and the 'caviar'. Decorate with lemon and parsley. *Serves 6.*

Danish Liverpâté

Dansk leverpostej

Liverpâté, home-made or bought, is extensively used for Danish open sandwiches and on the Cold Table. As a starter it is served slightly warm with crisply fried streaky bacon and fried mushrooms accompanied by toast.

300g (10oz) pig's liver	2.5ml ($\frac{1}{2}$ tsp) ground
250g (8oz) streaky bacon	cloves
(in one piece) or	2.5ml ($\frac{1}{2}$ tsp) allspice
fat pork	25g (1oz) butter
$\frac{1}{2}$ medium-sized onion	25g (1oz) flour
15ml (1 tbsp) chopped	300ml ($\frac{1}{2}$ pint) milk
anchovies	1 egg
5ml (1 tsp) salt	250g (8oz) streaky bacon
2.5ml ($\frac{1}{2}$ tsp) pepper	rashers (optional)

Mince the liver, streaky bacon and onion twice. Add the chopped anchovies, blend thoroughly and add all the seasonings.

Melt the butter in a saucepan, add the flour and cook gently over a low heat for 1 minute, then gradually stir in the milk, beating continuously. Bring to the boil and cook for 2–3 minutes. Remove the pan from the heat and blend in the liver mixture. Bind with the beaten egg.

Pour into a greased small loaf tin (which can be lined with streaky rashers). Cover with foil or greased greaseproof paper and place in a large roasting tin with approximately 2.5cm (1in) cold water. Place in the centre of a preheated oven, 160°C(325°F)/Gas 3, for 1–1$\frac{1}{2}$ hours. The pâté is cooked when a stainless steel skewer comes away clean.

When cooked remove from the oven and cool with a heavy weight on top. Leave until quite cold before turning out. This pâté can be frozen.

Fish Dishes

No Danes live more than twenty-five miles from the sea, and they are accustomed to eating fish which is plentiful and relatively inexpensive. Both salt and freshwater fish are eaten. Herrings, mackerel, cod and plaice are favourites but there is great variety — flounder, turbot, halibut, sole, trout, salmon and shellfish are all readily available.

Traditionally, the fishmonger keeps his fish alive in large water tanks until required by his customers. That way the fish is always impeccably fresh. In fact, Danes use the expression 'as fresh as a fish' where others might say 'as fresh as a daisy'.

Fishing is a national pastime as well as a commercial industry. Denmark is a coarse fisherman's paradise, with angling competitions on an international scale being arranged every year. Jutland is famous for its trout fishing and the excellent sea fishing attracts many visitors.

Years ago the fishing grounds were found near home. Now the boats go farther afield and in consequence Denmark today has a large frozen fish industry. Younger Danes are quite accustomed to eating frozen fish, which would have been unheard of in their grandparents' day.

Fish is preserved by smoking and salting or a combination of salting and drying as well as being canned and frozen. Smoked trout, mackerel, halibut and salmon are popular as toppings for smørrebrød or served on their own. Dried cod or plaice, although not so fine as the luxury smoked fishes, are very good indeed.

Danes also love shellfish — oysters, lobsters and crabs, and especially shrimps which are caught in great quantities in the summertime or may come from the arctic waters of Greenland, Denmark's largest province. A piece of smørrebrød with tiny freshly cooked shrimps and a glass of lager in Copenhagen's Tivoli Gardens is one of the treats of a Danish summer, although, alas, an expensive one.

The most popular ways of serving fish are lightly boiled, accompanied by melted butter or a cold herb butter, or fried in butter with the pan juices poured over. To fry fish in butter, heat the fat in the pan and add the fish when the butter begins to foam but before the browning stage is reached. The addition of 5ml (1 tsp) cooking oil to each 25g (1oz) butter in the pan will prevent burning without detracting from the buttery flavour of the cooked dish.

Fresh dill, tarragon, parsley and chives are commonly used in sauces to accompany fish.

New Year's Eve Cod
Nytårstorsk

January is the month for cod dinners. The fish must be boiled so carefully that the flesh lies in broad, chalk-white flakes, and served with quantities of melted butter and a hot mustard sauce that makes one's eyes water.

1.4kg (3lb) cod (whole fish)	30ml (2 tbsp) vinegar to 1 litre (2 pints) water
25g (1oz) salt	

Clean the cod and cut it into steaks about 4cm (1½in) thick. Sprinkle with half the salt and leave for 15 minutes. Rinse the fish. Add the remaining salt and measured vinegar to the measured water in a pan, bring to the boil and add the fish. Place the lid on the saucepan and bring the fish gently to the boil. Turn off heat and let the fish stand, with the lid still tightly closed, for about 10 minutes. Before serving, place the fish on kitchen paper to drain.

If you have a fish kettle, the cod may be served whole. Clean it and fill the stomach with potatoes to reform the shape (they will not be cooked when the fish is served, so extra potatoes must be prepared). Leave on the head and set a whole lemon in its mouth before bringing the dish to table.

Good accompaniments are boiled potatoes, chopped hard-boiled egg, grated horseradish, and chopped parsley. *Serves 6–8.* (Illustration page 24.)

Boiled Plaice with Parsley Sauce Kogt rødspætte med persillesauce

Go to a fish restaurant in Jutland in the summertime and you may be served with a huge plaice, thick on the shoulder and very filling. A few plain boiled potatoes, melted butter and parsley sauce will accompany this dish.

Plaice are also fried in butter. If the whole fish is too big for the pan, cut it in pieces through the backbone. This is quicker than filleting, and keeps the special flavour of fish cooked on the bone.

1-kg (2-lb) plaice (whole)	*25g (1oz) salt*
1 litre (1¾ pints) water	*2 bayleaves*

PARSLEY SAUCE:

25g (1oz) butter	*15–30ml (1–2 tbsp) finely*
25g (1oz) flour	*chopped parsley*
300ml (½ pint) milk, or	*salt and pepper*
milk and fish stock	

Clean the plaice, cutting off the fins and heads. Wash but do not soak it. Place the fish in cold salted water with the bayleaves. Bring gently to the boil, then simmer for approximately 5–10 minutes depending on the thickness of the fish. Strain and reserve the stock, and keep the fish hot.

To make the parsley sauce, melt the butter, stir in the flour and cook for 1–2 minutes without colouring. Remove from the heat and gradually add the milk or milk and reserved stock, stirring until smooth. Return to the heat and bring to the boil, stirring constantly. When the sauce has thickened, cook for a further 1–2 minutes, then add parsley and seasoning.

Serve the plaice with plain boiled potatoes, melted butter and parsley sauce. *Serves 4.*

Fried Plaice with Shrimps
Stegt rødspætte med rejer

Small fillets of plaice are suitable for this dish. Allow 175–250g (6–8oz) fish per person.

500g (1lb) plaice fillets	*100g (4oz) peeled and*
1 egg	*cooked shrimps*
15ml (1 tbsp) water	*15ml (1 tbsp) chopped*
dried breadcrumbs	*parsley*
100g (4oz) butter	*½ lemon*

Wash and dry the fish fillets. Beat the egg with the water. Dip each fillet in the egg mixture and then coat each side with the breadcrumbs. Leave for about 20 minutes before cooking; a little longer will do no harm. Melt 50g (2oz) of the butter in a frying pan following the guidance on frying with butter on page 25. Fry the fillets about 2–3 minutes on both sides until golden brown. Keep them hot.

Melt 25g (1oz) of the remaining butter in a separate pan. Drain and dry the shrimps if canned or bottled ones are being used. Fry them until thoroughly hot and spoon them over the fillets. Add the last of the butter to the pan and heat until browned. Mix in the chopped parsley and pour mixture over the fish. Decorate with slices of the lemon. *Serves 2.*

Plaice and Mushrooms
Rødspætte med champignon

8 plaice fillets	*250g (8oz) button*
salt and pepper	*mushrooms*
1 egg, beaten	*150ml (¼ pint) soured*
dried breadcrumbs	*cream*
100g (4oz butter)	*15ml (1 tbsp) tomato*
	purée

Lightly season the plaice fillets, dip them first in egg and then in breadcrumbs, and then put them in a well buttered ovenproof dish. Dot with 50g (2oz) butter, and bake in the oven at 190°C(375°F)/Gas 5 for 15–20 minutes until the fish is golden. Remove from oven.

Meanwhile, lightly cook prepared mushrooms in the remaining butter, then stir in the soured cream mixed with some tomato purée. Season to taste, pour the sauce over the fish and return to the oven for a few minutes. Serve with creamed potatoes. *Serves 4.*

Fish Gratin

Fiskegratin

750g (1½lb) fish fillets,   salt
  plaice or lemon sole

SAUCE:
40g (1½oz) butter   1 egg yolk
40g (1½oz) flour   salt and pepper
300ml (½ pint) milk   15–30ml (1–2 tbsp)
30ml (2 tbsp) white wine   grated cheese
juice of ¼ lemon   25g (1oz) breadcrumbs

Rinse and dry the fillets, put them in the bottom of a buttered ovenproof dish, and season with a little salt. Make up a sauce using the butter, flour and milk. Stir in the white wine and lemon juice, and fold in the lightly beaten egg yolk. Season to taste. Pour the mixture over the fish, mix the cheese and breadcrumbs and sprinkle over. Bake the gratin in the oven at 180°C(350°F)/Gas 4 for 20–30 minutes. The sauce can be varied with the addition of truffles, mushrooms, lobster or capers.
  Serve with French bread and butter. *Serves 4.*

Dried Jutlanders

Tørrede jyder

Here's a treat to look out for if you go up to the northernmost point of Jutland where the Kattegat meets the Skagerak. In the summertime fishermen salt small plaice or flounder and hang them out in pairs on a line to dry in the brisk summer air. Should you be lucky enough to be given some for a present, this is how to cook them.

1 or 2 'Dried Jutlanders'   butter for frying
  per person

Wash the fish, put them in cold water and bring them slowly to the boil. Simmer for 2–3 minutes depending on size, then drain and dry the fish. Melt plenty of butter in a frying pan and when the foaming subsides, put in the dried fish and fry both sides until the fins are crisp. Eat piping hot with rye bread and butter.
  Local people are reputed to eat the 'Dried Jutlanders' with their fingers but visitors usually prefer to use a knife and fork!

Fried Cod's Roe

Stegt torskerogn

Canned cod's roe is an excellent standby for a snack, or as a starter when guests are unexpectedly present. If fresh cod's roe is used, simmer it gently in salted water for approximately 30 minutes before frying it. Smoked cod's roe is not used in this way.

200-g (7-oz) can cod's roe   50g (2oz) butter

Slice the roe thinly into eight pieces. Fry the slices on both sides in the butter until golden brown. Arrange the slices so they overlap on a dish sprinkled with some chopped parsley or gherkins and serve with rémoulade sauce (page 94). Alternatively serve with grilled or fried bacon rashers. *Serves 3–4.*

Sole with Mock Hollandaise Sauce Søtunge med forloren Hollandaisesauce

6–8 fillets sole, skinned   1 small onion
150ml (¼ pint) water   1 bayleaf
5ml (1 tsp) tarragon   bouquet garni
  vinegar

SAUCE:
reserved cooking liquid   10ml (2 tsp) tarragon
milk   vinegar
40g (1½oz) butter   1 egg yolk
25g (1oz) flour   seasoning

Season and roll the fillets with the skinned side inside. Bake in an ovenproof dish with the water, vinegar, sliced onion, bayleaf, and bouquet garni at 190°C (375°F)/Gas 5, on the centre shelf, for 15–20 minutes. Pour off and reserve the stock and keep the fish hot.
  Make the stock up to 300ml (½ pint) with milk. Melt 25g (1oz) butter in small pan, add the flour, stir and cook 2 minutes. Gradually add the stock, stirring until smooth. Remove from heat. Stir in the vinegar and remaining butter, and quickly beat in the egg yolk. Cook gently for 1 minute more. Taste and season. If liked, add a little cream. Pour sauce over fish.
Serves 6–8 as a starter; 3–4 as a main course.

Blend the flour and milk, beat in the eggs and season. Skin and bone the mackerel and cut it in small pieces. Melt the butter in a frying pan and heat until just turning brown. Pour in the egg mixture and cook over a fairly high heat until set, lifting the edges occasionally. When nearly cooked through (about 5 minutes) arrange the pieces of smoked mackerel on top. Cook until set, about 1–2 minutes more. Remove the pan from the stove and garnish the top of the egg cake with chopped spring onions and radishes. Serve immediately straight from the pan.   *Serves 4.*

Bachelor's Supper
Ungkarlens ret

2 small plaice or dabs	*1 onion*
100g (4oz) butter	*2 large tomatoes*
1 sprig dill or chopped parsley	*salt and pepper*

Wash and dry the fish. Liberally butter a thick frying pan and add the fish together with dill or chopped parsley and chopped onion. Put tomato slices on the fish, season with salt and pepper and add remaining butter. Pour in 30ml (2 tbsp) water, cover and steam the plaice for 15 minutes. Serve with boiled potatoes or French bread.   *Serves 2.*

Summer Egg Cake
Sommer-æggekage

This is a variation of the better-known Bacon and Egg Cake. It is often served in Copenhagen during the summertime when mackerel is cheap and plentiful.

15ml (1 tbsp) flour	*250g (8oz) smoked mackerel*
90ml (6 tbsp) milk	
4 eggs	*15g ($\frac{1}{2}$oz) butter*
salt and pepper	*4 spring onions, chopped*
	8 radishes, chopped

Prawn Omelette
Æggekage med rejer

Greenland is famous for the quality of the shrimps and prawns which come from the arctic waters around its shores. Spare a thought for that distant land when serving this delicious omelette.

4 eggs	*1 small chopped onion*
200g (7oz) Greenland prawns or fresh peeled cooked prawns	*2–3 tomatoes, quartered*
	75g (3oz) diced Danbo cheese
75g (3oz) butter	*45ml (3 tbsp) water*
100g (4oz) mushrooms, peeled and sliced	*parsley*

Break the eggs into a bowl and beat them lightly. Drain the prawns. Melt 50g (2oz) of the butter in a pan and gently sauté the mushrooms, onion and tomatoes until tender. Add the prawns and diced cheese and cook together gently for a further 2–3 minutes to heat. Take a clean omelette pan and melt the remaining butter until it just begins to brown. Quickly mix the cold water into the eggs, pour the mixture into the omelette pan and cook fairly quickly, drawing the mixture away from the sides from time to time. When just setting, add sautéd vegetables and prawns on one side of the omelette. Fold over and dish up immediately on a hot serving dish, garnished with chopped parsley. *Serves 4.*

Prawn Omelette

Fried Eel with Potatoes

Stegt ål med stuvede kartofler

Some old Danish advice on the preparation of fish ran as follows: 'You should fry eel the way you lead ladies through town (i.e. slowly), but herring the way you chase whores out of town' (i.e. quickly).

500g (1lb) eel	750g (1½lb) new potatoes
1 egg, beaten	15g (½oz) flour
breadcrumbs	300ml (½ pint) milk
100g (4oz) butter	salt and pepper

Split and skin the eel and cut it in pieces about 6–7cm (2½in) long. Coat the pieces with egg and breadcrumbs. Fry them in the butter (keeping back 15g (½oz) for the sauce) for 15–30 minutes according to thickness. Wash the potatoes and boil them without peeling until just tender. Drain and leave to cool slightly before removing the skins.

Melt the remaining 15g (½oz) butter, stir in the flour and cook for 1 minute. Gradually stir in milk, bring to the boil and cook for 5 minutes. The sauce should not be too thick. Add the peeled potatoes, cutting larger ones into even sizes if necessary. Season with salt and pepper and reheat carefully without overcooking. Chopped chives or parsley are sometimes added to the sauce. Serve the fried eel pieces with the potatoes in the sauce. *Serves 4.*

Oysters

Østers

In ancient times, oysters were quite a common food. We know this because archaeologists have discovered several hundred mounds of oyster shells in Denmark, some of them in the Limfjord area, which date back to the early Stone Age. These shell heaps have been diagnosed as 'kitchen middens' and are the refuse of innumerable meals eaten by Stone Age man. Today Danes have a more varied diet and Limfjord oysters, though now world famous, have become a luxury.

Fresh oysters are served on the half-shell with a squeeze of lemon and a little pepper and salt. With them go slices of the close-textured Danish rye bread.

Fish Frikadeller

Fiskefrikadeller

Fish was once the cheapest protein food in Denmark and every fishmonger sold minced fish as a matter of course. Cod or pike were usually used, or a combination of both. Fish *frikadeller* have a softer consistency than those made of meat and are slightly flatter.

500g (1lb) fresh cod or other white fish fillets	2.5-5ml (½–1 tsp) curry powder (optional)
25g (1oz) onion	2.5ml (½ tsp) baking powder
5ml (1 tsp) salt	
100g (4oz) plain flour	300ml (½ pint) milk
1 egg	butter for frying
white pepper	

Remove skin and any bone from the fish, and cut the flesh into strips. Mince the fish 2 or 3 times with the onion. Stir in the salt, flour, egg (well beaten), pepper, curry powder if used and baking powder. Stir in half the milk and allow to stand in a cool place for 5 minutes. Blend in the remaining milk and allow to stand for 20 minutes more.

Melt the butter in a frying pan and shape the mixture using a dessertspoon dipped in the butter so the *frikadeller* are slightly rounded and egg shaped. They will flatten slightly in the cooking. Fry them in the butter for 4–5 minutes on either side. Serve piping hot with peas and carrots in sauce (page 67) and boiled potatoes. *Serves 4.*

Cheesy Trout

Ostepaneret ørred

1 egg, beaten	75g (3oz) Samsoe cheese, grated
45ml (3 tbsp) milk	
50g (2oz) fresh breadcrumbs	salt and cayenne pepper
	4 medium trout, cleaned
	75g (3oz) butter, melted

Preheat oven to 220°C(425°F)/Gas 7. Blend egg and milk. Combine breadcrumbs with 25g (1oz) grated cheese. Season with salt and pepper. Dip fish first in the egg mixture, then in the cheesy crumbs. Place in an ovenproof serving dish, pour over the melted butter, and add the remaining cheese. Bake for 15–20 minutes. *Serves 4.*

Fish Balls

Fiskeboller

These tiny fish dumplings are usually bought ready-made in cans, but they can be made at home. They are used in fish or tomato soups and to 'stretch' more expensive fish like shrimps or crab in filling *tarteletter* cases (page 22).

500g (1lb) white fish
  (e.g. whiting), skinned
  and boned
2.5ml (½ tsp) salt

25g (1oz) flour
1 egg white
150ml (¼ pint) milk

Mince the raw fish finely (3 times through the mincer), then mix all the ingredients together and stir well. Allow to stand for 15 minutes. The mixture should be rather slack.

Boil water in a large saucepan. Form small fish balls using a small teaspoon or egg spoon, drop them into boiling water, and simmer for 3 minutes. Make a few at a time, lifting them out with a slotted spoon as they are cooked. Serve with tomato soup or with a sauce in *tarteletter* cases. *Makes 30.*

Fish Fillets with Leeks

Fiskefileter med porregarniture

250g (8oz) leeks
50g (2oz) butter
10ml (2 tsp) cornflour
150ml (¼ pint) single
  cream or top of milk

500g (1lb) cod or
  haddock fillets
pinch salt and pepper

Prepare the leeks, discarding the green tops. Wash them well and cut them into thin slices. Melt the butter and sauté the leeks without browning until almost tender. Blend the cornflour with a little of the cream or milk, and add this to remainder. Stir the cream mixture into the leeks. Put the fish fillets in the bottom of a buttered ovenproof dish, season, and spoon the leek mixture over. Cook in a preheated oven at 180°C (350°F)/Gas 4 for 20–30 minutes. *Serves 4.*

Lumpfish Roe 'Caviar'

'Kaviar' af stenbiderrogn

One nice plus that the Danish hostess has in planning her menus is a relatively inexpensive but very acceptable substitute for caviar. This 'mock caviar', as it is usually called, comes from the roe of the lumpfish caught in the Limfjord and off the shores of Iceland and Greenland. The eggs are the colour of sand when freshly caught. Then they are thoroughly rinsed to separate them, salted and coloured black or red, and packed in glass jars. They make an attractive *hors d'oeuvre* or garnish.

MOCK CAVIAR ON TOAST

4 slices buttered toast
100-g (3½-oz) jar mock
  caviar
1 tomato

little parsley
1 lemon, washed and cut
  in quarters lengthwise

Prepare the buttered slices of toast and just before serving spoon the caviar on to the slices, decorate with a small slice of tomato and a parsley sprig. Put the quartered lemon on top.

Another way to serve mock caviar is to prepare it as above, but replace the garnish on each slice of toast with a large onion ring. Put a raw egg yolk in each ring and serve.

When the caviar is put out for guests to help themselves, the egg yolks are presented in half an egg shell held upright in a bowl of coarse sea salt or ordinary salt.

Other serving suggestions for mock caviar will be found on pages 75 and 86.

Herring Collation
Sildeanretning

Salt herrings and herrings in various marinades are often served as a first course, one or more kinds being put out in separate dishes on the table. Salt herrings are not easy to come by in many countries but jars of pickled, marinated herrings can usually be found in delicatessen shops. Rollmops may be substituted but do not have quite the same softness as pickled, marinated herring.

SPICED SAUCES TO SERVE WITH MARINATED HERRINGS

These sauces should be chilled and served in little bowls as an accompaniment to herrings for lunch or for a buffet party.

For the **basic sauce,** simply mix together the following ingredients:

150ml ($\frac{1}{4}$ pint) soured cream; 2.5ml ($\frac{1}{2}$ tsp) white wine vinegar; 2.5ml ($\frac{1}{2}$ tsp) sugar; pinch salt; 2.5ml ($\frac{1}{2}$ tsp) French mustard; 2.5ml ($\frac{1}{2}$ tsp) grated onion; and (optional) a dash of monosodium glutamate.

For a **tomato sauce,** mix *1 portion of the basic sauce with 10ml (2 tsp) tomato purée.*

For a **curry sauce,** mix *1 portion of the basic sauce with 5ml (1 tsp) curry powder and 2.5ml ($\frac{1}{2}$ tsp) sugar.*

To make a **dill sauce,** mix *1 portion of the basic sauce with 45ml (3 tbsp) finely cut dill and 2.5ml ($\frac{1}{2}$ tsp) sugar.*

For a **horseradish sauce,** mix *1 portion of the basic sauce with 20ml (4 tsp) grated horseradish and 5ml (1 tsp) sugar.*

Sunday Herrings
Søndagssild

325-g (11-oz) jar marinated herrings	*5–10ml (1–2 tsp) sugar*
milk	*pepper*
1 onion	*150ml ($\frac{1}{4}$ pint) soured cream*
1 eating apple	*cress*
juice of $\frac{1}{2}$ lemon	*paprika*

Drain the marinade from the herrings and steep them in milk for several hours. Drain and lay them in a dish. Grate the onion and dice the apple, putting it immediately into the lemon juice to prevent browning. Add sugar and a little pepper and lastly stir in the soured cream. Coat the herrings with the mixture and decorate with cress and paprika.

32

Fried Herrings with Dill

Stegte sild med dild

Herrings with roes are called fat herring and those without are known as empty herring.

1 herring per person	*flour for dusting*
salt and pepper	*butter for frying*
4 small sprigs fresh dill	
(or 2.5ml ($\frac{1}{2}$ tsp) dried	
dill) for each fish	

Split the herrings and remove the backbones, or buy them ready filleted from the fishmonger. Season inside the fish with salt and pepper, and a sprig of fresh dill or pinch of the dried herb. Close each fish with a piece of cocktail stick. Turn the fish in flour and fry them until crisp in plenty of butter. Serve with sautéd potatoes and fried onion rings.

Marinated Fried Herrings

Stegte sild i marinade

The Scottish saying 'of all the fish in the sea the herring is king' expresses a sentiment the Danes share. They love to eat herrings fried or marinated or, as in this recipe, treated both ways.

8 small fresh herrings	*300ml ($\frac{1}{2}$ pint) water*
30ml (2 tbsp) flour	*90ml (6 tbsp) sugar*
2.5ml ($\frac{1}{2}$ tsp) salt	*1 bayleaf*
2.5ml ($\frac{1}{2}$ tsp) pepper	*6 peppercorns*
butter for frying	*1 medium-sized onion*
300ml ($\frac{1}{2}$ pint) cider	
vinegar	

Split the herrings and remove the backbones. Turn the fish in the flour, salt and pepper and fry them in butter until golden brown.

Bring the vinegar, water and sugar to the boil, then let the mixture cool. Place the fried herrings in a dish with the bayleaf, peppercorns and the onion cut into thin rings. Add the vinegar marinade and leave dish for about 6 hours.

For the Cold Table, serve the herrings on a platter with brown bread and butter; as *smørrebrød*, drain the fish and serve them on brown buttered bread, garnished with raw onion rings.

Creamed Salted Herrings

Saltsild med fløde-porresauce

In times past, plain salted herrings were the standard farm breakfast, served with buttered rye bread. Something a little fancier may be preferred today.

4 salted herring fillets	*25g (1oz) sugar*
200ml (7fl oz) soured	*dill, cress and parsley,*
cream	*chopped, to garnish*
juice of 1 lemon	

Skin, bone and clean the herrings if necessary. Soak the fillets in milk or water for 24 hours. Mix the cream with the lemon juice and sugar. Drain and dry the fillets and cut them into small pieces. Put them in a dish and pour over the soured cream. Garnish thickly with the chopped green herbs.

TO MARINATE SALT HERRINGS

4 medium-sized salted	*125g (4$\frac{1}{2}$oz) sugar*
herrings	*few peppercorns*
600ml–1.2 litres	*3 bayleaves*
(1–2 pints) milk and	*1 or 2 onions cut into*
water	*rings*
300ml ($\frac{1}{2}$ pint) white wine	
vinegar	

Skin, bone and clean the herrings. Soak them in the milk and water for about 8 hours. Put the fillets in a shallow glass dish. Mix up all the remaining ingredients and pour this marinade over the fish. Leave overnight. Serve on *smørrebrød* or with plain boiled potatoes.

Meat and Poultry

The Danish housewife is well served with meats of all kinds by her butcher. Pork is the most popular and of excellent quality, as one would expect in a country famous for its bacon and meat exports. Beef, veal and offal are readily available. There is some lamb, all kinds of poultry and game, and many interesting kinds of sausages.

The standard of butchery is high and many butchers attend the national Meat Trade School, a sort of finishing school for butchers, where they study the techniques of hygiene as well as correct handling and cutting of meat. Butchers have a real pride in their craft and this results in a first-class service in their shops and the most splendid displays of stylishly cut meat in supermarkets.

Pork is often wrapped with a sprig of bayleaf inside ready to season it which looks most attractive, and there may even be a printed label with cooking tips alongside the price ticket. This fastidious preparation gives the housewife economical joints with no waste and saves time in the kitchen.

Even though Denmark is a prosperous country, for most people family meals must still be prepared with an eye to economy. Danish cooks are adept at making interesting dishes with minced meat and in using up left-overs on *smørrebrød* or in a soufflé-like preparation called 'gratin'.

The 'little warm dish' is an interesting feature. These are luncheon dishes usually served without vegetables after a few *smørrebrød*, or as part of the Cold Table.

There is no tradition of a Sunday roast followed by cold meat on Monday, because left-overs are used on *smørrebrød* or in made-up dishes. The meat is served differently too. Joints are carved in the kitchen, not at the table. The sliced meat is then arranged on a big serving dish surrounded by the cooked vegetables and looks most handsome when brought to the table. The dish is passed round for each person to help himself.

Roast Beef (page 36)

35

Only small portions are taken as it is customary to pass the meat at least once more for second helpings. A good rich gravy or sauce will accompany the meat or the vegetables may be served in a sauce instead. Fruit or cheese usually follows the meat dish rather than a pudding.

For convenience, the recipes in this chapter are based on meat cuts available in British shops. The Danish butcher cuts meat rather differently, as can be seen occasionally in the illustrations.

Joint of Roast Beef
Oksesteg

A lot of young beef is eaten in Denmark, but this recipe is for a traditional roast where the meat has been well hung.

2-kg (4-lb) joint of beef suitable for roasting	50g (2oz) butter 10ml (2 tsp) salt

Wrap the meat in aluminium foil greased with butter. Roast in the oven at 190°C(375°F)/Gas 5 for about 1½ hours. Remove foil. Rub the joint well with salt. Raise the oven temperature slightly, and replace the joint for a short time until it has browned.

Serve with glazed onions, sugar-browned potatoes, boiled potatoes, pickled cucumbers, cranberries and gravy made from the pan juices. *Serves 6–8.* (Illustration page 34.)

Hamburgers with Onion
Hakkebøf med løg

These Danish hamburgers are quickly fried so that the outside is dark and crisp and the centre slightly pink. Fried onions are served piled on top. Rich brown gravy, boiled potatoes and perhaps peas and carrots in sauce would complete the dish. Fried eggs are sometimes served on top of the hamburgers.

250g (8oz) onions butter for frying 500g (1lb) best quality minced beef salt and pepper	10–15ml (2–3 tsp) flour 300ml (½ pint) water or stock gravy browning

Peel and slice the onions and fry them until brown in butter. Put them aside to keep warm. Season the meat with salt and pepper and form it into large round cakes, about 100g (4oz) each. Melt some butter in the pan in which the onions were fried and quickly fry the hamburgers, about 4 minutes on each side.

Arrange the cooked hamburgers on a dish, with the hot fried onions on top. Stir the flour into the pan juices, add the stock and a drop of gravy browning if the colour is too pale. Cook for 2 minutes to thicken. Serve with the hamburgers and onions. *Serves 4.*

Skipper's Hotpot
Skipperlabskovs

There should be rather more potatoes than meat in this traditional stew, which is always cooked on top of the stove.

500–750g (1–1½lb) chuck steak or stewing veal 750g (1½lb) floury potatoes 1 large onion	300–450ml (½–¾ pint) water salt bayleaf few peppercorns approx. 50g (2oz) butter

Cube the meat, potatoes and onion. Boil the water and add the meat and onion. Skim and add remaining ingredients, cover and cook for 1½ hours until all ingredients are tender. The potatoes must be cooked to a mash so that they thicken the gravy. Serve with chopped parsley, rye bread and butter. *Serves 4.*

Beef Ragout
Okseragout

500–750g (1–1½lb) stewing steak	250g (8oz) carrots
4 rashers streaky bacon	250g (8oz) leeks
50g (2oz) butter	45ml (3 tbsp) tomato purée
450ml (¾ pint) stock	5ml (1 tsp) sugar
5ml (1 tsp) paprika	45ml (3 tbsp) cream
5ml (1 tsp) salt	chopped parsley
5ml (1 tsp) pepper	

Cut the meat into cubes and chop the bacon. Lightly fry in the butter. Add stock and seasonings, cover and simmer for about 2 hours at low heat until tender.

Prepare the vegetables, cut them into small pieces and add with the tomato purée to the meat. Simmer for a further 20 minutes. Stir in sugar and cream. Sprinkle with chopped parsley and serve with French bread.

To vary this stew, add ¼ celeriac and 2 large onions instead of the carrots and leeks. The remaining celeriac can be used raw in a vegetable salad.

This dish freezes well, so it's easy to make twice the amount and put half in the freezer. It will probably need extra seasoning when re-heated. *Serves 4–5.* (Illustration page 42.)

Liver and Bacon
Stegt lever med bacon

8 rashers streaky bacon	salt and pepper
375g (12oz) lamb or pig's liver	4 tomatoes, halved
flour	parsley
	1 lemon

Fry the rashers slowly to extract the fat and get them nice and crisp. Put them to one side to keep hot. Dip the slices of liver in seasoned flour and fry them lightly in the bacon fat on both sides, adding a little lard if necessary. Add the cooked liver to the bacon and keep warm. Lastly fry the halved tomatoes. Serve all together in a dish garnished with chopped parsley and the lemon cut in wedges. *Serves 4.* (Illustration page 42.)

Biksemad
Biksemad

The seasoning for this popular dish is 'English Sauce', the name the Danes use for Worcestershire sauce. The late King Frederik of Denmark is said to have eaten *biksemad* every week made, as his chef has explained, with fillet of beef. The proportion of meat to potatoes should be about one to two.

500g (1lb) potatoes, cooked	250g (8oz) onions, sliced
225g (8oz) cooked meat (beef, pork, etc.)	100g (4oz) lard
	Worcestershire sauce
	2–3 eggs

Cut the potatoes and meat into small cubes. Fry the onions until golden brown in some of the lard and set aside. Melt more lard and fry the potatoes until golden brown. Keep these hot with the onions. Add more fat to pan if required and heat the meat, turning it to prevent the pieces burning. When the meat is hot, return fried onions and potatoes to the pan, mix all together and heat if necessary. Sprinkle the mixture well with Worcestershire sauce, then transfer to a serving dish and keep hot. Quickly fry the eggs, put them on the *biksemad*, and bring the dish at once to the table. *Serves 2–3.*

Henne Strand Pork Chops
Henne Strand-koteletter

In the summer Danes love to spend time in their summer houses by the sea or in the country. They live plainly, cutting down on housework and cooking, staying out in the sun and air. This simple pork chop recipe is the type of meal served in the summer months.

4 thin pork chops	1 large onion, cubed
50g (2oz) butter	salt and pepper
3 apples, cubed	little curry powder

Brown the chops gently on both sides in a little of the butter. Put them to one side in an ovenproof dish. Fry the apple and onion in remaining butter. Add salt, pepper and curry powder. Place on top of the chops and bake in the oven for 20 minutes at 200°C (400°F)/Gas 6. *Serves 2–4.*

Pork with Apples
Svinekød med æble

500g (1lb) streaky pork   1kg (2lb) red-skinned
* or bacon chops   eating apples*
50g (2oz) sugar

Place the meat in a heated frying pan over a gentle heat. Pour the fat off once or twice while frying so that the meat becomes crisp. Take the pork or bacon out of the pan and keep it warm.

Wash the apples, but do not peel them. Remove stalks and cores and slice the fruit. Place the sliced apple in the pan with a little of the reserved fat and fry until tender. Sprinkle a little sugar over the apples, and place the fried slices on a dish beside the meat. Serve hot, with fried onion.

Use any left-overs as a topping for *smørrebrød*, using buttered rye bread as the base.   *Serves 4.*

Pork with Caper Sauce
Svinekød i kaperssauce

1-kg (2-lb) blade of pork   6 whole peppercorns
1 onion   50g (2oz) butter
1 leek   50g (2oz) flour
4–5 carrots   600ml (1 pint) stock
¼ celeriac   (from meat)
5ml (1 tsp) salt   30ml (2 tbsp) capers
1 bayleaf   5ml (1 tsp) sugar

Cut the rind off the meat and place the pork in a pan. Cover with water, bring to the boil, and skim. Add the prepared vegetables, season, and simmer the joint gently for about 1½ hours. The vegetables should be removed when they are cooked, and kept warm. Drain the meat and keep hot.

For the sauce, melt the butter in a pan and add the flour. Cook for 1 minute. Add 600ml (1 pint) of the cooking liquid to the sauce, allow to thicken and cook 3–4 minutes. Add the capers and sugar.

Slice the pork on to the serving dish and surround with the hot vegetables. Coat with a little sauce, and hand the rest separately.   *Serves 4.*

Roast Loin of Pork
Flæskesteg

A favourite not just at Christmas time but all the year round, pork with crackling means much to a Dane. Just how they get their crackling so crisp is described here.

Recipes for sugar-browned potatoes and red cabbage to serve with it are on pages 66 and 67.

1.5-kg (3¼-lb) loin of pork
   with rind
salt

100g (4oz) prunes,
   pre-soaked and stoned
2 small cooking apples

Ask the butcher to score the rind finely or do it at home using a very sharp knife. Preheat the oven to 220°C (425°F)/Gas 7. Cook the joint with the rind down in a roasting pan with just enough water to cover the rind only. Roast for 20 minutes in this way, then take out the joint and rub the rind with plenty of salt. Return joint to oven, rind side up, for a further 25 minutes until the rind begins to bubble. Turn oven temperature down to 150°C(300°F)/Gas 2 for 45 minutes, adding the prunes and apples (peeled and quartered) to the pan juices for the final 30 minutes' cooking time.

Make a gravy with the pan juices and serve the pork with the prunes and apples, sugar-browned potatoes and red cabbage.   *Serves 6.*

Curried Pork Chops
Koteletter i karrysauce

4–6 pork chops
4 onions
4 cooking apples
75g (3oz) butter
15ml (1 tbsp) curry
   powder
450ml (¾ pint) stock

50g (2oz) dried apricots,
   chopped
15ml (1 tbsp) chutney
salt
sugar to taste
juice of 1 lemon

Brown the chops on both sides in a frying pan, using a little extra fat if necessary. Put them in an ovenproof dish. Peel and dice the onions and apples and cook them gently in the butter until onion is soft, about 5 minutes. Add curry powder, stirring well, and fry 1–2 minutes more to cook the curry powder. Stir in the stock and other ingredients, bring to the boil, then pour over the chops. Cover the dish with foil and cook in the oven at 200°C(400°F)/Gas 6 for about ½ hour. Serve with boiled rice.   *Serves 4.*

Stuffed Pork Tenderloin
Svinemørbrod med fyld

This is a typically Danish dish for special occasions and has a marvellous sauce to go with it. Tenderloins of pork are rather variable in size, so you may have to adjust the cooking time if the ones you buy are either very plump or long and thin. If you have not got a frying pan large enough to brown the meat in one piece, it can be cut in two.

10–12 prunes, stoned	*50g (2oz) butter*
1 apple	*105ml (7 tbsp) water*
2 pork tenderloins,	*25g (1oz) flour*
about 750g (1½lb)	*200ml (7fl oz) milk or*
in weight	*cream*

Put the prunes to soak in a little hot water. Peel and slice the apple and put the slices in water to stop them discolouring. Put the pieces of tenderloin on a work surface and make a small slit right down the centre of each, not too deep, and open them up, pressing them out flat with the hand.

Drain the prunes, keeping the juice. Put the prunes and slices of apple along one of the tenderloins. Cover with the other, putting the thick end of one to the thin end of the other. Tie with string in three or four places, and close the ends with cocktail sticks.

Melt the butter in a frying pan until it begins to foam. Put in the stuffed tenderloin and brown it well, about 5 minutes on each side. Add the water. Cover the pan and simmer on low heat for 30–40 minutes.

Take out the cooked meat and keep it hot. Mix the flour with approximately 90ml (6 tbsp) of the prune water and stir it into the pan juices. Cook through. Add enough liquid to give a fairly thick sauce using the cream or milk, or a combination of both, to make about 300ml (½ pint).

Extra prunes and apples can be cooked in the pan around the tenderloin. Serve the tenderloin sliced, garnished with sugar-browned potatoes and red or buttered cabbage. Hand sauce separately. *Serves 4.* (Illustration page 42.)

Hamburgerryg
Hamburgerryg

Hamburgerryg is lightly salted and smoked pork loin, a great speciality for a dinner party, completely lean and delicately flavoured.

750g (1½ lb) Danish	*whipped butter sauce*
smoked pork loin	*or melted butter sauce*
(hamburgerryg)	*(page 74)*
vegetables (see method)	

Place the *hamburgerryg* in a saucepan of water, bring it to the boil, then simmer the meat gently for 10–15 minutes, turn off the heat, and leave in the hot water a further 10 minutes. Cut the meat in half if it is too big for the saucepan. This will not spoil the final appearance as it must be sliced before going to the table.

Serve with a medley of plain boiled new season's vegetables – cauliflower sprigs, new carrots and peas, and a mixture of plain boiled and sugar-browned potatoes. The meat should be thickly sliced and reformed into its original long sausage shape in the centre of a large serving platter with the vegetables ranged around. Serve immediately, letting guests help themselves. Whipped or melted butter sauce is served with the vegetables.

As a variation, the boiled *hamburgerryg* can be transferred to the oven for 10 minutes, coated with a little sugar and some pineapple slices and basted with the pineapple juice to glaze.

It may also be fried. Cut the raw *hamburgerryg* into 0.5-cm (¼-in) slices, dip each slice in seasoned flour and then in egg white and fry them in butter for about 4 minutes, turning once. Serve with peas and carrots in sauce (page 67) and potatoes.

Thin slices of uncooked *hamburgerryg* can be served with melon as an *hors d'oeuvre* or on *smørrebrød*. *Serves 4–6.*

Fried Meat Balls
Frikadeller

Well-made *frikadeller* are delicious, inexpensive and Denmark's national meat dish. Everyone eats and enjoys them and everyone has his own special recipe for making them. The meat should be finely minced and put through the mincer more than once to get the required soft texture. The meat used can be all pork, or a mixture of pork and veal or pork and beef. *Frikadeller* should be shaped with a tablespoon or dessertspoon to achieve the correct round but slightly pointed shape.

There are nearly as many recipes for *frikadeller* as there are cooks in Denmark. For instance some cooks consider that mixing with soda water gives *frikadeller* a lighter texture while others use stale breadcrumbs in place of flour. Three recipes with small variations are given here.

approx. 450ml ($\frac{3}{4}$ pint) milk	*2 egg whites or 1 whole egg*
100g (3$\frac{1}{2}$oz) flour	*10ml (2 tsp) salt*
750g (1$\frac{1}{2}$lb) minced lean meat (pork and beef)	*2.5ml ($\frac{1}{2}$ tsp) pepper*
1 onion, grated	*100g (3$\frac{1}{2}$oz) butter (for frying)*

Gradually mix together the milk and flour. Add the minced meat, grated onion, egg whites, salt and pepper. Stir this forcemeat thoroughly and leave for about 1 hour before frying.

Melt the butter in a heavy frying pan and when brown dip a tablespoon in the butter. Shape a spoonful of the mixture with the spoon and put it into the butter in the pan. Continue until all meat is shaped into oblong balls. Fry for 6–7 minutes and turn to fry for the same length of time on the other side.

Serve with either white potatoes, cold potato salad or vegetables. If served for lunch or snacks the meat balls can be shaped with a dessertspoon instead of a tablespoon to make them smaller. *Serves 4–6.* (Illustration page 42.)

Spiced Frikadeller
Krydrede frikadeller

The addition of allspice or nutmeg gives a subtle flavour to this recipe. If you are new to these spices it is wise to bear in mind that allspice is rather hot and peppery and nutmeg can be very pungent. Use them cautiously if you are not certain how much you will like them.

250g (8oz) minced beef	*1 small grated onion*
250g (8oz) minced pork	*150ml ($\frac{1}{4}$ pint) milk*
30ml (2 tbsp) flour	*1 egg*
2.5ml ($\frac{1}{2}$ tsp) salt	*butter for frying*
pinch pepper	
2.5ml ($\frac{1}{2}$ tsp) ground allspice or nutmeg	

Mix the meat with flour, seasoning and grated onion. Add milk and egg and stir well. Shape the mixture into little oblong balls with a spoon dipped in the melted butter. Fry the *frikadeller* slowly in the butter until brown on all sides.

As a supper meal, serve hot with potatoes and creamed spinach; for *smørrebrød*, serve cold, cut in slices on buttered brown bread with lettuce and beetroot; and for the Cold Table, serve hot or cold with pickled beetroot and gherkins. *Serves 4.* (Illustration page 42.)

South Jutland Meatballs
Sønderjydske frikadeller

This is an old recipe from South Jutland where the cooked meat is given added flavour by the addition of a little smoked bacon. When cooked meat is made into meat balls, the dish is called *Døde Frikadeller* – dead *frikadeller*!

225g (8oz) cooked meat	*2 slices white bread*
100g (4oz) smoked streaky bacon	*2 eggs*
	pepper and salt
1 onion, sliced	*butter for frying*

Mince the meat with the bacon and onion. Soak the bread in water, squeeze it and mix it with the meat. Beat the eggs lightly and add them to the meat mixture. Season with salt and pepper, shape and cook the *frikadeller* as in the first recipe. *Serves 3–4.*

Beef Ragout (page 37)

Stuffed Pork Tenderloin (page 40)

Liver and Bacon (page 37)

Frikadeller (page 40)

Duckling with Cherry Sauce
And med kirsebærsauce

2–2.5-kg (4–5-lb)
  duckling
½ lemon
sprig thyme
salt and pepper
454-g (1-lb) can pitted
  black cherries

15ml (1 tbsp) cornflour
1 miniature bottle
  Cherry Heering
lemon and watercress
  for garnish

Place the giblets in a small pan, cover with water, and cook gently for about 20 minutes.

Place ½ lemon and the thyme in the body of the bird. Season with salt and pepper. Prick the skin all over, taking care not to pierce the flesh. Weigh, and roast the duckling for 25 minutes per 500g (1lb) at 180°C(350°F)/Gas 4. Prick once during cooking.

Drain the cherries, and make the juice up to 300ml (½ pint) with the giblet stock.

Remove duck to a serving dish and keep hot. Reserve the lemon. Strain off the fat from the pan. Blend a little of the juice and stock with the cornflour. Add this to the roasting pan and cook, stirring, until sauce clears. Add the Cherry Heering and half the cherries. Season and squeeze in lemon juice.

Garnish the duck with lemon and watercress and serve the sauce separately. *Serves 4.*

Easter Chicken Casserole
Påskekylling med æggarniture

This is an appropriate dish to serve at Easter because of the attractive egg garnish.

1.4-kg (3-lb) chicken
6 small onions, peeled
50g (2oz) butter
30ml (2 tbsp) chopped
  parsley
600ml (1 pint) chicken
  stock

250g (8oz) mushrooms
salt and pepper
225-g (8-oz) packet frozen
  peas
2 eggs
30ml (2 tbsp) milk
30ml (2 tbsp) cornflour

Joint the chicken, and fry the joints and onions in the butter until lightly browned. Add 15ml (1 tbsp) parsley, the stock, sliced mushrooms and seasoning. Cover and simmer gently for 35 minutes, adding the peas for the last 10 minutes. Towards the end of cooking time beat the eggs and milk together, season the mixture, pour it into an omelette pan with a little butter, and cook until firm.

Put the chicken and vegetables on a heated serving dish and keep warm. Thicken the cooking liquor with cornflour blended with a little water. Cut the cooked egg into strips. Pour the gravy over chicken, garnish with the egg strips and the remaining chopped parsley. *Serves 4.*

43

Pot~roasted Chicken

Grydestegt kylling

This is how Danish cooks roast chickens on top of the stove, in a large thick-bottomed cooking pot.

1.4-kg (3-lb) chicken
5ml (1 tsp) salt
pinch pepper
75g (3oz) butter
150ml (¼ pint) stock or
   water
150ml (¼ pint) single
   cream
10ml (2 tsp) redcurrant
   jelly
30ml (2 tbsp) flour

Clean and wash the chicken. Dry it and season inside with salt and pepper. Place 25g (1oz) butter inside the chicken. Melt the remaining butter in a heavy pan and carefully brown the chicken on all sides until golden brown. Now add the hot stock or water and cook, covered, over a gentle heat for 45 minutes. Take the chicken out of the pan and keep it hot. Add the cream and redcurrant jelly to the juice from the chicken. Mix the flour until smooth with a little cold water and add to the gravy. Heat gently, stirring, for 5 minutes, and season to taste.   *Serves 4.*

Chicken with Horseradish Sauce **Kylling i peberrodssauce**

25g (1oz) butter
25g (1oz) flour
450ml (¾ pint) milk
   (or milk and left-over
   chicken broth)
150ml (¼ pint) double
   cream
60ml (4 tbsp) grated
   horseradish
salt
sugar
1 boiled chicken (see
   Chicken Broth, page 18)
parsley

Melt the butter in a pan and add the flour. Allow to cook for 1 minute without browning. Add the milk a little at a time, allowing the sauce to thicken. Add the cream, bring to the boil and cook for 5 minutes. Add horseradish, salt and sugar to taste.

Carve the chicken, add to the hot sauce, and heat through on top of the stove. Sprinkle with chopped parsley before serving.   *Serves 4.*

Tarragon Chicken

Estragon-kyllinger

1 chicken, about
   1.4kg (3lb)
75g (3oz) butter
5ml (1 tsp) salt
2.5ml (½ tsp) pepper
20ml (4 tsp) dried
   tarragon or a little
   fresh tarragon
30ml (2 tbsp) lemon
   juice
300ml (½ pint) stock
300ml (½ pint) double
   cream
parsley

Clean, rinse and dry the chicken and cut it into 4 pieces. Remove the tips of the wings. Brown the joints in butter and sprinkle with salt and pepper. Put the dried tarragon in lemon juice about ½ hour before frying to release the flavour. Add these, stock and cream to the saucepan when the joints are brown. Cover and simmer for 35 minutes until tender.

Put the chicken pieces on a serving dish, strain the sauce and pour it over the chicken. Sprinkle with chopped parsley.   *Serves 4.*

Roast Goose

Gåsesteg

225g (8oz) prunes
1 goose, about 4kg (9lb)
250g (8oz) apples
15ml (1 tbsp) salt
pinch pepper
15ml (1 tbsp) sugar
600ml (1 pint) boiling
   stock or water
45ml (3 tbsp) flour
gravy browning

Wash the prunes and put them to soak the day before. Clean and wash the goose, and dry it well. Wash and peel the apples, and cut them into slices. Mix the salt and pepper and rub it into the inside of the goose. Sprinkle the apples and stoned prunes with a little sugar and stuff the goose with them. Secure the cavity with a skewer or sew the skin together. Rub a little salt on the outside of the goose, and place it in a moderately hot oven, 190°C(375°F)/Gas 5, on one of the lowest shelves for about 20 minutes to brown. Pour away the fat and then pour the boiling stock or water into the pan.

Roast for at least 3 hours at 160°C(325°F)/Gas 3, with the back up for 1 hour and breast up for the remainder of the time.

During the last ½ hour of the cooking time, remove the dripping and gravy from the roasting pan, and turn the oven up slightly to brown and crisp the skin again.

Strain the gravy and remove the fat. Measure 600ml (1 pint) gravy into a saucepan. Stir the flour to a thin paste with a little cold water and mix it into the gravy. Boil for 10 minutes, add salt and pepper to taste, and a little browning.

Serve the goose with browned and boiled potatoes and red cabbage. *Serves 12.*

Easter Veal
Påskekalv

1-kg (2-lb) leg or shoulder of veal	pinch dried thyme
15 small onions	bunch of parsley
15 whole cloves	10ml (2 tsp) salt
250g (8oz) carrots	50g (2oz) butter
2 sticks celery	1 medium-sized onion, chopped
1 litre (2 pints) water	
1 bayleaf	125g (4oz) small mushrooms

SAUCE:

40g (1½oz) butter	600ml (1 pint) stock reserved from cooking veal
40g (1½oz) flour	

Cut the meat into 2.5-cm (1-in) lean cubes. Stud each small onion with a clove. Peel and slice the carrots and chop the celery sticks.

Place these vegetables with the meat and water in a saucepan. Add bayleaf, thyme, most of the parsley and salt and simmer for about ¾ hour until the meat is tender. Strain the meat and vegetables and keep hot. Retain the cooking liquid but discard herbs.

Melt the butter in a frying pan and add the chopped onion. Fry gently until transparent and then add the washed mushrooms. Cook together for a few minutes.

Make the sauce by melting the 40g (1½oz) butter and stirring in the flour. Gradually add about 600ml (1 pint) of the meat stock and cook, stirring until the sauce has thickened.

Add the veal, cooked vegetables and fried onion and mushrooms to the sauce. Heat thoroughly and serve garnished with remaining parsley. *Serves 4.*

Veal in Dill
Kalv i dild

750-g (1½-lb) shoulder of veal	5 ml (1 tsp) salt
10 white peppercorns	1½ bunches dill or 10ml 2 tsp) dried dillweed
2 bayleaves	

SAUCE:

40g (1½oz) butter	150ml (¼ pint) soured cream
40g (1½oz) flour	
300ml (½ pint) stock	dill leaves or 10ml (2 tsp) dried dillweed
300ml (½ pint) milk	

Place the meat in a saucepan with just enough water to cover. Bring to the boil and skim carefully. Add peppercorns, bayleaves, salt and the dried dill or stalks of the fresh dill, retaining the leaves for the sauce. Simmer until tender, approximately 1 hour. Strain the stock and reserve for the sauce. Keep the meat hot.

To make the sauce, melt the butter in a heavy saucepan and add the flour while stirring. Add stock, milk and soured cream and bring to the boil. If the sauce is too thick, more stock can be added. Mix finely cut dill leaves or the dried herb into the sauce and season carefully. To serve, slice the meat and pour the sauce over.

This dish can be served with small boiled potatoes sprinkled with fresh dill if available. A less rich sauce can be made by using all milk. *Serves 6.*

Bacon Cookery

As most people know, good bacon has 'Danish' written all over it in the shape of the famous strip-mark **DANISH** which is stamped on the rind.

No other meat is quite so versatile as bacon. Uniquely flavoured, and easy to cook, bacon can be fried, grilled, boiled or roasted with equal ease. Served hot or cold it tastes right at any time of day.

Bacon and eggs are a classic dish the world over. Bacon sandwiches are as well known as cucumber or smoked salmon ones and a piece of boiled bacon is a weekly mainstay in many homes. A little bacon enhances the flavour of stews and flans, and used with poultry it protects and flavours the delicate breast meat. In its cold form it is a wonderful ingredient for *réchauffé* dishes.

But it is a strange fact that this versatile meat is little used in Danish cooking even though, for over a hundred years, a good deal of the bacon on British tables has come from Denmark. The Danish love of fresh pork has come to be complemented by the British love of bacon and Danish farmers have learned to produce lean pigs which provide both fresh meat and top quality bacon.

Sophisticated methods of curing Danish bacon produce the characteristic mild flavour and consistent control of saltiness. Standards of hygiene and quality are rigorously maintained so that the bacon is fresher, less salty and better suited to quick and easy preparation.

Most of the recipes in this section are of modern origin and take into account the wider use of rashers for meals other than breakfast and the more imaginative cooking of bacon joints which has emerged in recent years. All have the flavour of the Danish cuisine through the choice of Danish bacon as their main ingredient and the many Danish garnishes and serving ideas which have been added.

Buying Bacon

Bacon is widely available as it is sold by grocers as well as by butchers and supermarkets. There is a good choice of cuts from rashers and steaks through to joints. It is usually sold boneless, which makes it an economical meat in terms of the price related to the number of meals that can be served. You will need to allow 175g (6oz) uncooked bacon per serving for most of the recipes.

Points to look for when buying bacon are a fresh appearance, firm white fat, and pink, firm lean areas. Bacon can be bought smoked and unsmoked. In the case of Danish bacon it is smoked in Britain to suit local tastes, or remains in its natural unsmoked state. There is a subtle difference in flavour and in storage qualities.

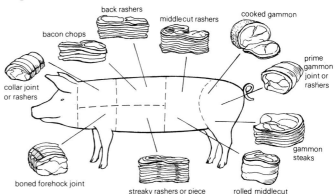

The bacon side is divided initially into three main sections: the gammon, the middlecut and the fore-end.

The gammon is the back leg of the pig and has finely textured meat with a delicate flavour. It can be further divided into *gammon joints, steaks* and *rashers*.

The middlecut is generally rashered, providing *back rashers* with a good 'eye' of lean, *streaky rashers* and *middlecut* or *through-cut rashers*.

Whole Roast Gammon (page 55)

The fore-end is the shoulder and neck area of the pig. The fore-end meat has more fat interspersed with it than the gammon and although not so finely textured, is both tender and well flavoured. The two main divisions of the fore-end are the *collar* and *forehock*. Collar bacon, which is also referred to as shoulder bacon, can be divided into smaller joints or rashered. A forehock of bacon can be bought whole on the bone or boned and rolled and divided into smaller joints

Storing Bacon

To enjoy bacon at its maximum freshness and flavour, joints and rashers should be cooked and eaten within a week of purchase, unless stored in a freezer. Because bacon is a cured meat it needs protection from the air and should be tightly wrapped in kitchen foil or cling film. Greaseproof paper should not be used as it is porous and allows the bacon to dry out. While there is little difference in the storage time between smoked and unsmoked bacon in the larder or refrigerator, in the freezer smoked bacon keeps longer than unsmoked.

Some bacon is vacuum-packed to extend its keeping quality. The Danish producers have their own brand called Danepak. Vacuum-packed bacon should be treated as fresh bacon once opened.

Larder or Cool Store Cupboard Well wrapped fresh joints and rashers will keep uncooked for 3–4 days; vacuum-packed bacon, up to 7 days.

Refrigerator Storage Uncooked fresh bacon rashers wrapped tightly in foil or cling film will keep for 7–8 days. Uncooked fresh bacon joints, well-wrapped, should be cooked within 5 days.

For vacuum-packed bacon joints and rashers follow the recommendation on the packet. Danepak bacon bought frozen will keep up to one month in the refrigerator.

Freezer Storage Uncooked fresh bacon can be frozen successfully but not for such long periods as fresh meat. It is important to remember that smoked bacon can be frozen for longer than unsmoked bacon. Bacon for the freezer should be really fresh – check with your retailer if in doubt.

To freeze fresh bacon, pack it first in kitchen foil, allowing ample coverage. Exclude as much air as possible and place each parcel of bacon in a polythene bag. Again exclude as much air as possible and clip or tie

the bag. Smoked bacon joints wrapped in foil and polythene will keep for 8 weeks; unsmoked bacon joints similarly wrapped will keep for 5 weeks.

Vacuum-packed bacon joints, smoked and unsmoked, will keep 20 weeks after the date-mark.

Freezer packs of Danepak are marked 'keep frozen, best before . . .' and allow up to 6 months' storage depending on date of purchase.

Thawing The more slowly bacon is thawed the better the quality of the meat will be when cooked, so thawing in the refrigerator is recommended. The wrapping material should be opened – or, in the case of a vacuum pack, the end cut off – on removal from the freezer. Remove wrappings completely as soon as possible during the thawing process. Frozen bacon should be cooked immediately it has thawed for the best results.

Cooked Bacon Joints do not freeze well, as a flavour change soon takes place. If it is necessary to freeze a piece of left-over bacon, the length of storage time should be no more than 2–3 weeks. Stews or dishes containing bacon, such as quiche lorraine, in which the bacon pieces are surrounded by a liquid, may be frozen for short periods but not more than 6 weeks.

Bacon Joints

Soaking This is no longer essential for long periods before cooking, as the milder Danish cure requires little or no soaking. If you still prefer to soak a bacon joint, 1–3 hours in cold water is sufficient for small joints, up to 8 hours for larger ones.

An alternative to soaking is to bring the bacon slowly to the boil in cold water, drain the joint and then continue with the chosen cooking method, but this is only practical for joints that fit easily into an average size saucepan.

Boiling This is the traditional method for cooking bacon joints, to serve either hot or cold. Use a saucepan large enough to hold the joint comfortably and deep enough to allow the joint to be covered completely with water. Wash and weigh the joint and calculate the cooking time at 20 minutes per 500g (1lb) plus 20 minutes over. Place the joint in the saucepan, cover with cold water, bring slowly to the boil and then reduce the heat to a gentle simmer. Time the cooking

Devilled Gammon Steaks (page 59)

Mustard-topped Streaky Bacon (page 51)

Old-fashioned Orange-glazed Bacon (page 54)

from this point. Keep the lid on during cooking and maintain a steady simmer, topping up with hot water to keep the joint covered.

A few bayleaves, black peppercorns and a tablespoon of demerara sugar or black treacle can be added to the cooking water for extra flavour. Wine, cider or the juice from canned fruit can be used in the same way.

At the end of the cooking time, drain the joint, allow to cool slightly and carefully remove the rind, either peeling it off or cutting it with a sharp knife.

The fat surface can then be glazed to give an attractive finish and add delicate flavour to the sliced meat. To do this, score the fat in a criss-cross design and spread a sugar-based glaze over it. Then place the joint in a hot oven for 10–15 minutes to allow the glaze to melt and colour. For a plainer finish, lightly browned breadcrumbs can be pressed into the fat surface.

Roasting   Most cuts of bacon, for instance gammon and fore-end joints, are delicious roasted. This method is particularly suitable for bigger joints which are often too large for saucepans. Whole forehocks and gammon on the bone can be foil-roasted, so as to preserve the maximum amount of moisture in the meat. Strictly speaking this method should be termed baking, as the joint is covered and not open roasted. At one time these large joints were baked in a flour and water paste but this has gradually been replaced by the use of foil. Bacon joints can also be open roasted and spit roasted. A meat thermometer can be used when roasting bacon joints, and is particularly helpful when cooking large joints such as a whole gammon. The inner temperature should never be below 70°C(160°F). Whether you want the temperature to rise higher than that will depend on how well cooked you wish the meat.

The following list provides general guidelines for roasting times in foil.

CUT AND WEIGHT	MINUTES PER 500g (1lb)	OVEN
Whole gammon on the bone 7.25–7.75kg (16–17lb)	20 minutes, plus 20 minutes extra	180°C(350°F)/ Gas 4
Gammon joints		
up to 1.4kg (3lb)	30 minutes	190°C(375°F)/
up to 2.75kg (6lb)	25 minutes	Gas 5
over 2.75kg (6lb)	20 minutes	
All other joints		
up to 1.4kg (3lb)	35 minutes	190°C(375°F)
up to 2.75kg (6lb)	30 minutes	Gas 5
over 2.75kg (6lb)	25 minutes	

Parboiling/Roasting   A combination of boiling and roasting produces a very good result. The use of the two methods takes a little longer, but the excellent texture and flavour of the cooked meat makes it worthwhile. It is also an ideal method to use when stuffing a bacon joint – suitable joints are middlecut or streaky (page 56). Calculate the cooking time as for roasting and boil for half the time, then transfer to the oven in foil for the remaining time.

Braising   Collar and forehock joints braised on a bed of vegetables make a lovely meal. They can be cooked in the oven or on the hob.

Pressure Cooking and Steaming   Small bacon joints under 1.5kg (3¼lb) in weight are best suited for these two methods.

Bacon Rashers

Bacon rashers are ideal for quick and easy meals at any time of day. Rashers can be cut from any part of the bacon side. Back rashers, the prime rashers for breakfast, are recognized by the good 'eye' of lean and small area of fat. Streaky rashers get their name from the way the lean and fat are distributed in long streaks. A good buy which combines both these rashers is called middlecut or through-cut. Here the back and streaky are sliced in one long rasher which can be cut in half before cooking. Rashers can be grilled or fried and take approximately 2–4 minutes, turning once.

Gammon Steaks

Gammon steaks can be grilled or fried in 10 minutes or prepared slowly in the oven. They generally weigh 100–225g (4–8oz) and are cut approximately 1cm ($\frac{1}{2}$in) thick. The larger steaks can be served as a single portion or cut in half to give 2 servings.

Bacon Chops

Bacon chops are thickly cut lean back rashers. They weigh between 100–175g (4–6oz) each, and are cut between 0.5–1cm ($\frac{1}{4}$–$\frac{1}{2}$in) thick. For serving allow 1 or 2 chops per person. They are cooked and served in much the same way as gammon steaks.

Marinated Bacon

$\frac{1}{2}$ bottle red wine
1 large onion, peeled and chopped
10ml (2 tsp) dried rosemary
10ml (2 tsp) dried thyme

fresh or dried parsley as available
1.25-kg (2$\frac{1}{2}$-lb) collar bacon, unsmoked

Heat the red wine, onion and herbs together. Put the bacon joint, without soaking, in a close-fitting bowl and pour over the cooled marinade. Ideally it should come well up the sides of the joint. Cover and leave in a cool place, turning once or twice, for 24 hours. When ready to cook, transfer the joint and marinade to a saucepan that fits the joint snugly and add sufficient water to bring the liquid over the top of the meat. Cover with a lid, bring to the boil, reduce heat and simmer for 20 minutes per 500g (1lb) and 20 minutes over.

Drain away the marinade and leave the joint to cool overnight before serving. Leave on the rind, which takes on an attractive dark colour from the wine and is soft and easy to carve.

Slice meat on a domestic rotary meat slicer or use a sharp knife to cut thin slices. The bacon will be really succulent and intriguingly flavoured by the marinade. Serve with salad and jacket potatoes. *Serves 6, cold and thinly sliced.*

Mustard-topped Streaky Bacon Joint

1.4-kg (3-lb) streaky bacon joint
1 small onion stuck with 4 cloves
1 bayleaf

45ml (3 tbsp) mustard
15ml (1 tbsp) brown sugar
50g (2oz) breadcrumbs
$\frac{1}{2}$–1 egg, beaten

Bring bacon to the boil in cold water. Drain and place joint in fresh cold water to cover. Add the onion stuck with cloves and the bayleaf. Bring to the boil again, reduce the heat and simmer for 20 minutes per 500g (1lb) plus 20 minutes.

Prepare the topping by mixing the dry ingredients together and binding them with the beaten egg. Remove the joint from the cooking liquid and place it in a roasting pan. Allow to cool slightly and remove the rind. Spread the mustard topping on the fat surface. Place in a hot oven, 200°C(400°F)/Gas 6, for 10–15 minutes until the top is crusty and golden. Serve hot or cold. *Serves 4–6.* (Illustration page 49.)

Boiled Bacon with Apricot Topping

1.25-kg (2$\frac{1}{2}$-lb) bacon joint
411-g (14$\frac{1}{2}$-oz) can apricots
30ml (2 tbsp) apricot juice

30ml (2 tbsp) cornflour
60ml (4 tbsp) demerara sugar
10ml (2 tsp) white vinegar

Weigh the joint and calculate the cooking time at 20 minutes per 500g (1lb) plus 20 minutes.

Bring the bacon to the boil in cold water. Drain and place joint in fresh cold water to which the canned apricot juice has been added. Bring to the boil, cover and simmer for calculated cooking time.

Gently mash the drained apricots with a fork. Blend the cornflour with a little cold water. Stir into the apricots and add remaining ingredients. Heat gently to dissolve sugar and cook to thicken and clear.

When the bacon is cooked, drain and remove the rind. Spread some sauce on top as a garnish, and serve the remaining sauce separately. *Serves 4–6.*

Celebration Gammon

A superb centrepiece for a party, to serve either hot or cold.

4.5-kg (10-lb) prime boned gammon with shank bone attached	30ml (2 tbsp) soft brown sugar
30ml (2 tbsp) made mustard	maraschino or glacé cherries
	long-stemmed cloves

Wash the joint thoroughly and soak in cold water for up to 3 hours. Calculate the cooking time at 20 minutes per 500g (1lb). Wrap the joint in foil and place it in a large roasting pan with a little water in the bottom of the pan. This prevents any fat from the joint from burning. Place the joint on the lowest shelf of the oven and bake at 190°C(375°F)/Gas 5.

Meanwhile, blend the mustard and sugar together. Remove the joint from the oven 20 minutes before the end of the cooking time, cut off the rind and brush the fat with the mustard mixture. Return it to the oven for the remaining 20 minutes, until just brown.

Halve the cherries and arrange them over the gammon, using the cloves to anchor them. If necessary use broken cocktail sticks and disguise these with cloves. *Serves 12–15.*

Spiced Bacon

1.25-kg (2½-lb) bacon joint	sprig rosemary
500g (1lb) cooking apples	15ml (1 tbsp) French mustard
600ml (1 pint) cider	10ml (2 tsp) demerara sugar
1 onion stuck with cloves	cloves
	12.5ml (2½ tsp) cornflour

Place the bacon joint in a saucepan and cover with cold water. Bring slowly to the boil, then discard water. Peel and slice the apples and put them in a saucepan with the cider, onion and rosemary. Place the joint on top. Cover with water and bring to the boil. Reduce heat to a gentle simmer and cook for 20 minutes per 500g (1lb) and 20 minutes over.

Remove the bacon joint from the cooking liquor and place it in a roasting tin. Mix together the mustard and sugar. Remove the rind, score the surface into diamond shapes, spread the mixture over the top fat, and stick with cloves. Bake in the oven at 200°C(400°F)/Gas 6 for 10 minutes.

For the gravy, drain the stock from the apples and reduce it by boiling to 450ml (¾ pint). Blend a little cornflour with cold water, add the hot stock, return to the pan, stir and boil to thicken.

Sieve the well-drained apples and onion, discarding the cloves and rosemary, and serve as an apple sauce with the bacon and gravy. Serve with cauliflower and Brussels sprouts. *Serves 4–6.*

Gala Gammon

1.8-kg (4-lb) middle gammon joint	60ml (4 tbsp) clear honey
bouquet garni	4 eating apples
2 carrots, peeled	juice ½ lemon
2 onions, peeled	1 orange
30ml (2 tbsp) fresh breadcrumbs	3 maraschino cherries
	little redcurrant jelly

Bring the gammon to the boil in cold water. Drain, and return joint to the pan with the bouquet garni, carrots and onions. Cover with fresh cold water, bring back to the boil, reduce heat and simmer for 20 minutes per 500g (1lb) and 20 minutes over, keeping pan covered. Transfer the joint to a roasting tin and remove any string and the rind. Mix together the breadcrumbs and honey and spread over the fat. Cook the joint in the oven at 220°C(425°F)/Gas 7 for 10 minutes to crisp the topping.

While the gammon is cooking, prepare the apples by cutting them in half across the core. Brush each cut surface with a little lemon juice and poach them gently in shallow water for 5 minutes. Drain and keep warm.

When the gammon is ready, garnish the joint with thin orange slices and cherries spiked together with frilly cocktail sticks, and the apple halves topped with a little redcurrant jelly.

Roast potatoes, forcemeat balls and green beans are vegetables which would go well with this dish. *Serves 6–8.*

Roast Whole Forehock

1 whole forehock on the bone, smoked or unsmoked, weighing 3.2–4kg (7–9lb)	5ml (1 tsp) dry mustard
	15ml (1 tbsp) demerara sugar
45ml (3 tbsp) apricot jam or marmalade or a mixture of both	10ml (2 tsp) wine vinegar
	pepper

Cut off the shank bone and reserve for Bacon Spread (page 54) or to use in soup. This leaves a forehock joint which can be boned before cooking or left with the bone in.

Weigh and wrap the joint in foil and calculate the cooking time at 25 minutes per 500g (1lb). Place joint in a roasting tin and cook at 190°C(375°F)/Gas 5 for the calculated time, less 30 minutes. Remove foil and take the rind off the joint. Mix the remaining ingredients together for the glaze and brush half of it over the meat. Return the joint to the oven and cook for the remaining ½ hour uncovered, spooning over the remaining glaze during cooking. Cut off and reserve the fatty end of the joint for *biksemad* (page 37) before taking the forehock to table. Serve with cauliflower and carrots. *Serves 8–10.*

Old~fashioned Orange~ glazed Bacon

Bacon joints used to be baked in a flour and water paste, which made them succulent and tender and prevented them from drying out. Today flour paste is rarely used and joints are baked in kitchen foil instead. Both methods are given here.

1.4-kg (3-lb) collar bacon joint	juice of 1 orange
50g (2oz) soft brown sugar	cloves
	1 small orange to garnish

Weigh the joint and calculate the cooking time at 30 minutes per 500g (1lb). Wash thoroughly in cold water.

If you are using kitchen foil, wrap the joint well, and roast it in the centre of a preheated 190°C(375°F)/Gas 5 oven for the calculated time.

Mix together the brown sugar and a little of the orange juice for the glaze; 20 minutes before the end of the cooking time, remove the joint from the oven, open the foil and strip away the rind. Score the fat surface in a criss-cross pattern. Pour the remaining orange juice over the joint and spread the glaze over the scored fat. Stud with cloves. Return the joint to the oven for the remaining cooking time to allow the glaze to brown. Use the foil to support the glazed surface uppermost.

To bake the joint in a flour and water paste
Sieve 450g (1lb) plain flour and mix to an elastic dough with 300ml ($\frac{1}{2}$ pint) water. Quantities may vary depending on the size of the joint. Roll the dough out evenly to a size large enough to enclose the joint. Place the joint on the dough and wrap completely, moisten the edges and press to seal. Place in a greased roasting tin and bake for calculated cooking time at 180°C (350°F)/Gas 4; 20 minutes before the end of the cooking time, remove the joint from the oven, break away the crust and glaze the joint as above. Alternatively, let the joint finish cooking in the paste covering. When it is cooked, remove the paste, strip off the rind and coat the fat surface with toasted breadcrumbs before serving.

Garnish with twists of fresh orange and serve with Duchesse potatoes. *Serves 4.* (Illustration page 49.)

Bacon Spread

1 forehock shank	pepper
10ml (2 tsp) grated onion	50g (2oz) butter
15ml (1 tbsp) chopped parsley	

Weigh the shank and calculate the cooking time, allowing 30 minutes per 500g (1lb) and 30 minutes over.

Cover the shank with cold water, bring slowly to the boil, reduce the heat and simmer until cooked. Remove from heat and cool.

Cut the rind and fat from the shank and finely mince the meat. Mix in the remaining ingredients and beat well until the mixture is smooth. Pack into a dish and, if liked, melt a little extra butter to pour over the top. Chill before serving in sandwiches or with toast.
Makes about 225g (8oz).

Whole Boiled Gammon

1 whole gammon, smoked or unsmoked, weighing 7.25–7.75kg (16–17lb)	2–3 bayleaves
	30ml (2 tbsp) demerara sugar
12 peppercorns	toasted breadcrumbs

A whole gammon can be boiled if a pan large enough to take a joint of this size is available. Calculate the cooking time at 15 minutes per 500g (1lb).

Place the joint in the cooking pan on top of the cooker. Cover the joint completely with cold water, add peppercorns, bayleaves and sugar. Cover the pan and bring slowly to the boil. This can take quite a long time, depending on the pan size and quantity of water used. Time the cooking period from when simmering point is reached. Keep the pan covered throughout cooking, checking once an hour to ensure that the level of water covering the joint is maintained. If necessary top up with boiling water from a kettle.

When cooking is completed allow the water to come off the boil before moving the pan. With assistance, move the pan from the stove and carefully drain the joint. Allow to cool for at least $\frac{1}{2}$ hour before removing the rind.

Coat the joint with buttered breadcrumbs as for the Whole Roast Gammon, or with lightly toasted breadcrumbs.

Cool, store in the refrigerator, and leave for 24 hours before carving. *Serves 20–25.*

Whole Roast Gammon

1 whole gammon, smoked or unsmoked, weighing approx. 7.25–7.75kg (16–17lb)

125–175g (4–6oz) melted butter
175–225g (6–8oz) soft white breadcrumbs

A whole gammon is easily roasted in the oven and will require a cooking time of 20 minutes per 500g (1lb) at 180°C(350°F)/Gas 4 plus 20 minutes. It should be at room temperature before roasting and can be soaked in cold water for up to 8 hours if wished. Wrap the joint in single foil and bake for calculated cooking time.

Remove the joint from the oven and open up the foil. Reset the oven to 220°C(425°F)/Gas 7. Carefully remove the rind from the joint and brush the fat lightly with some of the melted butter. Mix the breadcrumbs with a little of the remaining melted butter and press on to the fat surface. Baste the crumbs with any remaining butter so they are evenly coated. Return the gammon to the oven for an additional 20 minutes until the surface is lightly browned. *Serves 20–25 when cold.* (Illustration page 46.)

Tipsy Bake

2-kg (4½-lb) forehock or collar bacon
8 peppercorns
15ml (1 tbsp) demerara sugar
2 bayleaves
300ml (½ pint) white wine
15ml (1 tbsp) brandy
30ml (2 tbsp) black treacle

10ml (2 tsp) made mustard
30–45ml (2–3 tbsp) wine vinegar or white wine
15ml (1 tbsp) demerara sugar
25g (1oz) sultanas or raisins

Weigh the joint and calculate the cooking time at 30 minutes per 500g (1lb). Place the joint in a saucepan and cover with cold water. Add peppercorns, demerara sugar and bayleaves to the water and bring slowly to the boil. Reduce heat and simmer for half the calculated cooking time.

Prepare a baste by combining the 300ml (½ pint) white wine, brandy, treacle and mustard together in a small basin. Set oven at 190°C(375°F)/Gas 5. Drain the joint and strip away the rind. Score the fat and place the joint in a roasting tin. Baste with the prepared mixture and place the joint in the centre of the oven for the remaining cooking time, basting frequently.

Remove the joint from the roasting pan and keep hot. Add a little extra white wine or white wine vinegar to the remaining pan juices, blend together and sweeten to taste with demerara sugar. Add sultanas or raisins, heat thoroughly and serve separately. Serve the joint hot or cold. *Serves 8.*

Spit~roasted Bacon with Barbecue Relish

1.4–1.8kg (3–4lb) bacon joint
100g (4oz) brown sugar

juice of 1 small orange
cloves

Middle gammon or a piece of boned and rolled forehock are ideal for this recipe. Weigh the joint and calculate the cooking time at 25 minutes per 500g (1lb) for gammon and 30 minutes per 500g (1lb) for forehock. Place the joint in a saucepan and cover with cold water. Bring the joint to the boil, reduce heat and simmer for half the cooking time. Drain the joint, remove the rind and score the fat. Mix most of the sugar with a little of the orange juice.

Place the joint on a spit, press the sugar mixture on to the scored fat, and spike with cloves. Finish cooking at a medium heat, basting occasionally with the remaining sugar and orange juice.

If you do not have a spit attachment, the joint can be roasted in the oven at 190°C(375°F)/Gas 5 for the second half of the cooking time.

Serve with a barbecue relish (page 58). *Serves 4–8.*

Roast Sunday Gammon with Crackling

An unsmoked corner gammon joint which has a good rind surface is ideal for open roasting to produce a delicious crackling finish for a Sunday roast.

1.5-kg (3¼-lb) unsmoked corner gammon

Preheat the oven to 200°C(400°F)/Gas 6. Weigh the joint and calculate the cooking time at 30 minutes per 500g (1lb). Using a sharp knife, score the rind in a criss-cross pattern. Wash the joint thoroughly in cold water. If wished, soak the joint for 1–2 hours.

Place the joint on a piece of foil in a roasting pan and cover the lean areas with foil to protect them, leaving the scored rind surface uncovered. Add a little water to the bottom of the pan. Roast in the oven, on the centre shelf, for the calculated cooking time until the rind surface forms crisp crackling.   *Serves 4–5.*

Apricot~stuffed Streaky

1.8-kg (4-lb) piece streaky bacon	*100g (4oz) fresh breadcrumbs*
3–4 bayleaves	*1 stick celery, chopped*
100g (4oz) dried apricots	*15ml (2 tbsp) chopped parsley*
	1 egg

Weigh the joint and calculate the cooking time at 30 minutes per 500g (1lb). Divide the streaky joint in two equal pieces and bring to the boil in plenty of cold water. Add the bayleaves and simmer the joint for 20 minutes. Drain and cut off the rind.

Pour boiling water over the apricots and soak them for 10 minutes, reserve 2 for decoration and chop the rest. Mix the remaining ingredients with the apricots and spread the mixture on the rib side of one half of the bacon. Cover with the other half and score the top fat. Press the 2 pieces together, tie and wrap in foil. Bake in the oven at 180°C(350°F)/Gas 4 for remaining cooking time, opening the foil for the final 15 minutes to brown the top. Sprinkle on a little brown sugar to glaze. Decorate with reserved apricots and fresh bayleaves. *Serves 10–12, thinly sliced, when cold.*

Apricot-stuffed Streaky

Bacon Stewpot

225g (8oz) dried butter beans
750-g (1½-lb) unsmoked collar bacon or slipper joint
250g (8oz) leeks, sliced
40g (1½oz) butter
1 small onion, chopped
30ml (2 tbsp) plain flour
450ml (¾ pint) stock
125g (4oz) carrots
pepper

Soak the dried butter beans overnight in cold water, then drain and simmer them gently in fresh cold water for 30 minutes.

Remove the rind and any excess fat from the bacon and cut the meat into 2-cm (¾-in) dice. Place in pan of cold water and bring slowly to the boil, then discard the water and drain well on kitchen paper. Melt the butter in a saucepan, add the leeks and onion, and cook gently until soft but not brown. Stir in flour, gradually add stock and bring to the boil, stirring. Cook for 1 minute. Remove from the heat and add the carrots, peeled and sliced, the bacon, drained beans, and pepper. Cover and cook gently for 1¼ hours. Garnish with chopped parsley. *Serves 4.*

Braised Gammon

500–750g (1–1½lb) boneless middle gammon
15ml (1 tbsp) brown sugar
250g (8oz) tomatoes
250g (8oz) Spanish onions
pepper
125g (4oz) mushrooms
juice of ½ lemon
chopped parsley

Place the gammon in a pan of cold water and bring it slowly to the boil. Pour the water away, cut off the rind and score the fat in several places. Place the gammon in a shallow flameproof dish. Sprinkle with the sugar and place under a preheated grill to melt and brown. Remove skins from the tomatoes and chop the flesh coarsely. Peel and thinly slice the onions, and add them in layers with the tomatoes to the dish. Season with pepper.

Cover the dish with foil and cook for 1½–1¾ hours at 180°C(350°F)/Gas 4. Wash and slice the mushrooms and cook them in a little water with the lemon juice for about 3 minutes. Drain and use to garnish each end of the dish. Sprinkle chopped parsley over, and serve with Brussels sprouts and boiled potatoes. *Serves 4.*

Braised Gammon

Barbecue Relish

25g (1oz) butter
1 onion
396-g (14-oz) can peeled
    tomatoes
30ml (2 tbsp) cider
    vinegar

30ml (2 tbsp) demerara
    sugar
dash Worcestershire sauce
30ml (2 tbsp) sweet pickle
2.5ml ($\frac{1}{2}$ tsp) French
    mustard

Gently melt the butter, add the chopped onion and cook until soft, but without browning, for 5 minutes. Add remaining ingredients, bring to boil, reduce heat and simmer for 10 minutes. Serve either hot or cold.

Bacon Gravy

15ml (1 tbsp) pan juices
    from roast bacon joint
15ml (1 tbsp) flour

300ml ($\frac{1}{2}$ pint) vegetable
    stock or chicken stock
    cube with water
pepper
gravy browning

Retain the hot fat in the pan after removing the roast bacon joint. Stir in the flour well and brown the mixture a little over a gentle heat, stirring all the time. Gradually add the vegetable stock or chicken stock cube dissolved in boiling water. Bring gravy to the boil, season with a little pepper and add a drop or two of gravy browning to colour.

Casseroled Bacon Joint

1.25-kg (2$\frac{1}{2}$-lb) forehock
    joint
4 small onions
4 carrots

2 leeks, sliced
25g (1oz) lard
bouquet garni

Weigh the joint and calculate the cooking time at 35 minutes per 500g (1lb). Place the joint in a saucepan and cover with cold water. Bring slowly to the boil, then discard the water. Cover with fresh water and bring to the boil again. Reduce heat and simmer for half the calculated cooking time.

Prepare the vegetables and fry them gently in the lard for about 10 minutes. Place them in a deep ovenproof casserole. Drain bacon from pan and strip off the rind, retaining a little of the stock to cover the fried vegetables in the casserole. Place the bacon joint on the vegetables and add the bouquet garni. Cover the casserole with a lid and place the joint in the centre of a preheated oven, 180°C(350°F)/Gas 4. Twenty minutes before the remaining cooking time is completed remove the lid from the casserole to allow the fat surface of the joint to brown. Serve sliced, with the vegetables and thickened stock.   *Serves 4.*

Bacon Pudding

This is a recipe to serve in the cold weather. It can be steamed or pressure-cooked.

500g (1lb) gammon
    slipper
175g (6oz) self-raising
    flour
75g (3oz) prepared suet
pinch salt

50g (2oz) onion, chopped
50g (2oz) carrot, chopped
pinch dried mixed herbs
pepper
15ml (1 tbsp) flour

Remove the rind from the bacon and cut the meat into 1-cm ($\frac{1}{2}$-in) cubes. If you are going to steam the pudding, bring bacon to the boil in cold water, reduce the heat and simmer for 15 minutes. If you are using a pressure cooker, bring the bacon pieces to the boil in cold water, drain and replace in the cooker with fresh water to cover. Bring to *high* pressure and cook for 10 minutes, then reduce pressure.

Mix together the self-raising flour, suet, salt and 105ml (7 tbsp) water for the suet pastry. Cut off a quarter and keep it for the lid. Roll out the remainder and use to line an 850-ml (1$\frac{1}{2}$-pint) pudding basin. Drain the partly cooked bacon, mix it with the onion, carrot, herbs, some pepper and 15ml (1 tbsp) flour. Fill the basin with this mixture and pour in 200ml (7fl oz) water. Roll out the lid, damp the edges and place in position, sealing well. Cover with a double layer of greaseproof paper with a pleat in it, and tie with string.

To steam the dish, place basin in a saucepan with hot water reaching two-thirds up the side of the basin, or use a steamer. Cook for 2$\frac{1}{2}$ hours, checking the water level in the saucepan occasionally. Remove the paper and string, tie a napkin round the basin, stand it on a plate and serve with potatoes and vegetables.

If using a pressure cooker, put 1 litre (1$\frac{3}{4}$ pints) water in the pan and position the pudding on the trivet. Cover and bring slowly to *high* pressure. Cook 45 minutes, then reduce pressure at room temperature. Serve as for steaming method.   *Serves 4–6.*

Layered Gammon Steaks with Plum Sauce

8 gammon steaks, cut thin (approx. 50g (2oz) each)

STUFFING:

1 large onion
1 stick celery
100g (4oz) butter
2.5ml ($\frac{1}{2}$ tsp) ground nutmeg
15ml (1 tbsp) chopped parsley
25g (1oz) chopped hazelnuts (optional)

225g (8oz) fresh breadcrumbs
5ml (1 tsp) coriander powder
50g (2oz) seedless raisins
salt and pepper
2 eggs, well beaten

PLUM SAUCE:

500g (1lb) yellow or red plums
300ml ($\frac{1}{2}$ pint) white wine
10ml (2 tsp) tarragon vinegar

45ml (3 tbsp) clear honey
15ml (1 tbsp) cornflour

Remove rind from the gammon rashers. Prepare and chop the onion and celery and cook them slowly in 50g (2oz) of the butter. Remove from the heat and mix in remaining stuffing ingredients, except the reserved butter. Divide and spread the mixture evenly over four steaks. Cover each with the remaining steaks and press them together. Place layered steaks in a baking dish, dot with remaining butter, cover with foil and cook at 190°C(375°F)/Gas 5 for 35 minutes.

To make the sauce, stand the plums in hot water for about 2 minutes, then halve them and remove skin and stones. Simmer the fruit in the wine and vinegar until tender. Sieve or liquidize the fruit and liquor. Return to the pan, adding honey, and simmer without a lid to reduce by a quarter. Blend the cornflour with cold water and add a little hot liquid, then stir this into the pan. Bring to the boil, stirring, to thicken and clear. This will take about 2 minutes.

Arrange the layered steaks down the centre of a serving dish and garnish with tomatoes and peas or other vegetables. The sauce may be passed round separately or spooned over the layered steaks and garnished with chopped parsley. *Serves 4.*

Bacon, Egg and Mushroom Flan

PASTRY:

175g (6oz) plain flour
pinch salt
40g (1$\frac{1}{2}$oz) butter

40g (1$\frac{1}{2}$oz) lard
cold water to mix

FILLING:

1 small onion
25g (1oz) butter
125g (4oz) streaky bacon rashers

175g (6oz) mushrooms
2 eggs
150ml ($\frac{1}{4}$ pint) milk
salt and pepper

Sieve flour and salt and rub in the butter and lard. Mix with cold water to form a dough. Roll out the pastry to line a 20-cm (8-in) flan ring. Lightly prick the base and leave in a cool place to chill slightly. Set the oven at 200°C(400°F)/Gas 6.

To make the filling, chop and cook the onion in the butter until soft. De-rind and chop the bacon rashers. Wash and chop the mushrooms. Add both these to the onion and fry gently together for 5 minutes. Place this mixture in the flan case. Beat the eggs with milk, and season. Pour into the flan and cook for 35–40 minutes until the mixture is set and golden brown on top. Serve hot or cold with salad. *Serves 4.*

Devilled Gammon Steaks

2 175-g (6-oz) gammon steaks, smoked or unsmoked
little melted butter

French or English mustard
25g (1oz) demerara sugar
396-g (14-oz) can pineapple rings

Snip the rind on the gammon steaks to prevent them curling under the grill. Brush one side with a little melted butter and cook them under a fairly hot grill for 5 minutes. Turn the steaks over, brush with a little more butter and spread them with mustard to taste and some of the sugar. Grill for a further 5 minutes. Strain the juice from the pineapple and arrange two slices on each steak, sprinkle with remaining sugar and heat for a further 2 minutes. Garnish with tomatoes and sweetcorn. *Serves 2–4.* (Illustration page 49.)

Burning Love Braendende kaerlighed

This traditional Danish recipe is a delicious idea and very simple to prepare. Nobody seems to know why it has such a romantic name, but whatever the reason it makes a quick, enjoyable meal.

750g (1½lb) potatoes
milk
butter
salt and pepper

2 large onions
250g (8oz) streaky bacon
    rashers
little cooked beetroot
chopped parsley

Peel and boil the potatoes. When cooked, mash them with milk, butter, salt and pepper to taste. Keep them hot. Peel and slice the onions and cut the bacon rashers into small pieces, leaving the rind on. Gently fry the bacon pieces over a low heat until the fat begins to run, then increase heat and fry them until really crisp. Lift the bacon pieces out of the fat and keep them hot. Fry the onion in the bacon fat until soft and tender. When the onion is cooked, heap the hot potatoes on to a serving dish and arrange the crisply fried bacon and onions on top. Pour over any bacon fat left in the pan for extra flavour. Garnish with the chopped cooked beetroot and parsley and serve piping hot. *Serves 4.*

Bacon Breakfasts

Bacon rashers can be served any time of day, but as a breakfast dish they are unsurpassed. A different way to serve bacon in the morning, perhaps when guests are staying, is to grill or fry back rashers, washed mushrooms and halved tomatoes. Fry some ½ slices of bread, layer the rashers and fried bread down the centre of a serving dish, and surround them with the mushrooms and tomatoes.

Here are two other breakfast ideas, to suit all the family and give a nutritious start to a busy day.

Slimmer's Breakfast

Lean bacon can be used in calory-controlled diets and makes a sustaining meal at breakfast time.

	calories
½ grapefruit	20
1 grilled bacon rasher	122
1 grilled tomato	6
½ slice toast, buttered	79
tea or coffee with milk	16
	243

Vikings' Breakfast Platter

4 middlecut rashers
2 slices white bread

2 large tomatoes
2–4 eggs

Remove the bacon rinds, cut them into small pieces and fry to extract fat. Discard pieces. Add extra fat to the pan if necessary. Fry bread turning once. Remove from pan and keep hot. Gently fry the rashers with the halved tomatoes for 3–4 minutes until tender. Remove and keep hot. Break the eggs into the pan, spoon a little fat over the top and fry until just set and cooked. Serve immediately. *Serves 2–4.*

Fried Bacon Chops

Remove the rind from the chops and snip the fat at intervals. Fry the meat gently in its own fat or add a little butter or lard, allowing 5 minutes for each side. Arrange the cooked chops on a dish and garnish with fried mushrooms and tomato. Allow 1–2 175-g (6-oz) chops per person.

Crumbed Bacon Chops

Remove the rind and snip the fat at intervals. Dip the chops first in beaten egg and then in breadcrumbs. Use 50g (2oz) bread sauce crumbs and 1 beaten egg to coat 4 chops. Fry the breaded chops gently in butter for 10 minutes, turning once. Serve with new peas and potatoes. Allow 1–2 175-g (6-oz) chops per person.

Sweet and Sour Chops

Heat together 45ml (3 tbsp) tomato ketchup, 5ml (1 tsp) vinegar and 15ml (1 tbsp) brown sugar. Brush this mixture over 2 prepared bacon chops and cook them under a moderate grill for 5 minutes. Turn chops, brush again with tomato mixture, and cook for 5 more minutes. *Serves 1–2.*

Bacon Stuffing

You don't need a lot of bacon to make these delicious stuffings. The first one is particularly good with poultry.

125g (4oz) streaky bacon rashers
1 small onion
25g (1oz) butter
pepper

75g (3oz) fresh white breadcrumbs
30ml (2 tbsp) chopped parsley
beaten egg or milk

Remove the rind and cut the bacon into pieces. Peel and chop the onion. Cook the bacon and onion for about 4 minutes in the butter. Stir in the pepper, breadcrumbs, and chopped parsley. If necessary add a little beaten egg or milk to bind the ingredients together. Put the stuffing in the neck area of the chicken. Extra bacon rashers can be placed over the breast of the chicken during cooking to add flavour and keep the meat moist. *Makes enough to stuff the neck area of a 1.5-kg (3-lb) chicken.*

This rather richer stuffing is suitable for filling vegetables such as tomatoes and peppers.

100g (4oz) bacon rashers
1 small onion, chopped
15g ($\frac{1}{2}$oz) butter
2 mushrooms, washed and chopped

25g (1oz) fresh breadcrumbs or cooked rice
pinch dry mustard
few drops Worcestershire sauce
beaten egg

Remove the rind and chop the bacon rashers. Lightly fry the onion in the melted butter for 1–2 minutes. Add the mushrooms and chopped bacon and fry until onion is soft. Remove from heat. Add breadcrumbs, seasoning and Worcestershire sauce. Bind with beaten egg.

Use to stuff large tomatoes or green peppers. Cut off lids and remove the seeds. Wash the tomatoes and scald the green peppers for 5 minutes. Spoon the stuffing into the vegetables and place in a well-buttered ovenproof dish. Add a little water, cover with foil and bake for 15–20 minutes at 190°C(375°F)/Gas 5.

Bacon Rolls

These are an excellent garnish for poultry, or can be handed round on cocktail sticks at parties.

4–6 rashers of streaky bacon

Stretch the rashers with the back of a knife, halve them and roll them up. This enables the rashers to roll more easily and cook easily. Thread the bacon rolls on to skewers and cook under a medium grill or round a bacon joint, turning once.

Picnic Loaf

600-g (1¼-lb) collar joint or other lean bacon	*pepper*
50g (2oz) onion	*2.5ml (½ tsp) grated lemon rind*
50g (2oz) breadcrumbs	*1 egg*
15ml (1 tbsp) chopped parsley	*60ml (4 tbsp) stock*
2.5ml (½ tsp) dried mixed herbs	*3 rashers streaky bacon (optional)*

Bring the bacon to the boil in plenty of cold water and simmer for 10 minutes, or soak for 3 hours. Remove rind, fat and any gristle, then dice meat and mince it with the onion. Mix in remaining ingredients, except the bacon rashers. Grease a 500-g (1-lb) loaf tin and, if using the rashers, take off the rind and stretch them slightly to fit the tin. Fill tin with bacon mixture, press down well and cover with foil. Cook in a roasting tin half filled with water at 160°C(325°F)/Gas 3 for 1½ hours. Eat hot or cold.   *Makes 6–8 slices.*

Bacon and Egg Cake
Aeggekage med bacon

This is one of the few traditional bacon dishes to be found in Denmark. It is a very popular item on hotel and restaurant menus.

250g (8oz) streaky rashers	*salt and pepper*
15ml (1 tbsp) flour	*15g (½oz) butter*
90ml (6 tbsp) milk	*parsley or chives and*
4 eggs	*tomato to garnish*

Remove the rinds from the bacon rashers. Place the rashers on the grill pan and cook until golden brown and crisp (about 3–4 minutes). Meanwhile blend the flour and milk, beat in the eggs and season. Melt the butter in a frying pan and heat until just turning brown. Pour in the egg mixture and cook over a fairly high heat until set, lifting the edges occasionally. When cooked through, approximately 5–6 minutes, place the hot bacon rashers on top. Garnish with chopped chives or parsley and wedges of tomato, and serve straight from the pan.   *Serves 3–4.*

Gammon Slices in Tomato and Sherry Sauce

4–6 thick slices of cooked gammon or bacon joint	*298-g (10½-oz) can condensed tomato soup*
15g (½oz) butter	*pinch white pepper*
15g (½oz) flour	*90ml (6 tbsp) single cream or top of milk*
60ml (4 tbsp) dry sherry	*chopped parsley*

Place the bacon slices, overlapping, in a buttered casserole dish. Melt the 15g (½oz) butter in a saucepan and stir in the flour. Cook gently for 1 minute. Remove the pan from the heat and gradually stir in the sherry, tomato soup and pepper. Return to a low heat and cook, stirring constantly, until the sauce thickens. Remove from the heat and stir in the cream.

Pour the sauce over the meat. Cover with foil and bake at 190°C(375°F)/Gas 5 for 10–15 minutes until heated through.

Garnish with chopped parsley and serve with grilled mushrooms.   *Serves 4–6.*

Danish Risotto

2 medium-sized onions
1 stick celery
1 green pepper
50g (2oz) butter
175g (6oz) Patna rice
300ml ($\frac{1}{2}$ pint) stock or
  bouillon
50g (2oz) seedless raisins
5ml (1 tsp) salt
pinch pepper
225g (8oz) cooked bacon
225-g (8-oz) can
  pineapple pieces
225-g (8-oz) can sliced
  peaches, chopped
parsley chopped

Chop the onions and slice the celery finely. De-seed, wash and slice the peppers. Melt the butter in a heavy saucepan and cook the vegetables in the butter without browning. Add the rice and cook for 3–4 minutes until the rice has absorbed the butter and is slightly browned. Pour in 150ml ($\frac{1}{4}$ pint) stock, add raisins and seasoning and cook gently for 20–25 minutes, stirring occasionally with a fork and gradually adding the remaining stock.

Meanwhile, cut the cooked bacon into 0.5-cm ($\frac{1}{4}$-in) cubes, drain the pineapple, and drain and chop the peaches. Add these ingredients to the risotto 5 minutes before the end of cooking time. Garnish with chopped parsley and serve with a green salad. *Serves 4–6.*

Ham in Aspic

25g (1oz) gelatine
1 chicken stock cube
60ml (4 tbsp) sherry
10ml (2 tsp) lemon juice
5ml (1 tsp) vegetable
  extract
500g (1lb) cooked bacon
20 black grapes
2 peach halves (fresh or
  tinned)

Put the gelatine in a basin with a little cold water to soften, then stand the basin in hot water to dissolve the gelatine. Place the stock cube, sherry, lemon juice and vegetable extract in a measuring jug. Make up to 600ml (1 pint) with boiling water. Stir until the stock cube dissolves, then add the gelatine and allow liquid to cool slightly.

Cut the cooked bacon into 2.5-cm (1-in) dice. De-seed grapes and slice peaches. Rinse a 900-ml (1$\frac{1}{2}$-pint) ring mould. Place diced bacon, grapes, and peaches in the bottom. Pour over cooled gelatine mixture and place in

the refrigerator to set. Turn out on to a round plate. Rinse the plate in cold water beforehand as this will enable the aspic mould to be easily positioned. Garnish with watercress.

Eat within 1 day if kept at room temperature or 2 days if refrigerated. *Serves 6–8.*

Quick Ways with Left-overs

For a light luncheon dish, dice cold, cooked bacon from a joint, fry lightly in butter, then add to hot baked beans.

Fry chopped, cooked bacon with cold cooked potatoes and some onions, and top each serving with a poached egg.

Add cubed cooked bacon to a batter pudding seasoned with herbs.

Mince or finely chop cooked bacon and use as a filling for bacon and egg pie and savoury flans.

Mince cold cooked bacon finely and use it in a cheese and ham soufflé.

Add 225g (8oz) cooked bacon and 100g (4oz) lightly fried mushrooms to 600ml (1 pint) white sauce seasoned with salt, pepper, a little mustard, and 15ml (1 tbsp) sherry or white wine, if available. Serve with rice.

Mix cold chopped bacon with an equal quantity of mashed potato, add 30–45ml (2–3 tbsp) white breadcrumbs and season well. Bind with beaten egg and shape into round cakes with a little flour. Fry in hot fat until golden brown.

Dice 175g (6oz) cooked bacon, mix with 100g (4oz) grated potato and chopped onion. Season with thyme and pepper. Use to fill pasties made from 225g (8oz) shortcrust pastry.

Use sliced cooked bacon in sandwiches spread with mustard or sweet pickles.

Vegetables
and Salads

Vegetables and salads play an interesting role in the Danish way of eating, and the presentation of meat and fish dishes owes a good deal to them – especially the national specialities of *smørrebrød* and the Cold Table. They give the finishing touches to a meal, and provide the colour that is so important to Danish food.

Vegetables and fruits, both home-produced and flown in from warmer climes, are displayed immaculately cleaned and fresh in the shops and their sheer variety indicates that the people are accustomed to using them.

Good use is made of root vegetables as in other northern countries and because Danes are more faithful to the old ways they often use foodstuffs which town-dwellers in other lands no longer prepare themselves.

Danish cooks prefer small potatoes and the farmers grow the varieties that meet this demand. They are usually boiled first and then skinned. For festive occasions there are special varieties in Denmark known as 'asparagus' potatoes and 'egg yolk' potatoes, both names indicating the shape, i.e. long and narrow like an asparagus spear or round and yellowish like the yolk of an egg.

White and red cabbage, cauliflower, kale, spinach and Brussels sprouts are commonplace. Roots include onions and leeks, beetroot, celeriac. There are peas and beans, celery and asparagus and an abundance of salad vegetables – lettuce, mushrooms, tomatoes and cucumber, and radishes which are imaginatively used for decoration as well as flavour.

The taste of fresh herbs, especially dill, parsley and chives, is married with many dishes, or they are used as a garnish along with cress and watercress. Horseradish is highly regarded for its flavour and chervil makes a popular soup in the summer.

65

Potatoes in Sauce
Stuvede kartofler

This dish means simply boiled potatoes, served in a thin white sauce. Small waxy potatoes are best, but larger ones cut into small pieces will do so long as they are not overcooked. In Denmark this is often served with plain boiled ham.

750g (1½lb) small or new potatoes	450ml (¾ pint) milk or mixture of equal parts
40g (1½oz) butter	milk and potato stock
40g (1½oz) flour	salt and white pepper
	parsley or chives

Wash the potatoes and boil them until tender, about 15–20 minutes. Rinse them in cold water, leave a few minutes, peel off the skins and slice them thinly. Make up a white sauce with the butter, flour and liquid. Season with salt and pepper and nutmeg if liked. Turn the sliced potatoes in the sauce and let them heat through before serving. Sprinkle finely chopped parsley or chives on top.

In winter time, old potatoes are put in brown onion sauce made by frying a chopped onion with flour until browned and then adding the stock.   *Serves 4.*

Sugar~browned Potatoes
Brunede kartofler

In the old days it was customary to serve sugar-browned potatoes as a treat with plain boiled potatoes. Nowadays sugar-browned potatoes are often served on their own. They need not be new ones, but they should be small and firm.

750g (1½lb) small potatoes	25g (1oz) sugar
	25g (1oz) butter

Scrub the potatoes and boil them in their skins in salted water until just tender. Drain and peel.

Melt the sugar in a heavy frying pan over a gentle heat. When the sugar turns light brown around the edge, add the butter and stir until melted.

Rinse potatoes in cold water, tip them into the caramelized butter and shake the pan gently now and then until potatoes are nicely glazed and heated through. This will take about 10 minutes.   *Serves 4.*

Butter~browned Potatoes
Smørbrunede kartofler

50g (2oz) butter	salt
750g (1½lb) potatoes, cooked and sliced	parsley

Melt the butter in a large frying pan and let it brown slightly. Turn the potatoes in the butter and heat them through without overbrowning them. Put the potatoes into a serving dish, sprinkle them generously with coarse salt and finely chopped parsley.   *Serves 4.*

Sugar~browned Onions
Glaserede løg

500g (1lb) small onions	25g (1oz) butter
25g (1oz) sugar	

Peel and simmer the whole onions until tender. Melt the sugar in a frying pan until lightly caramelized, then add the butter. Rinse the onions in cold water. As soon as the butter in the pan begins to bubble in a light brown foam, put in the onions. Shake them gently in the pan until evenly coated with the caramel and a golden brown. Serve at once.   *Serves 4.*

Caramelized Carrots
Glaserede gulerødder

750g (1½lb) small new carrots	25g (1oz) sugar
	25g (1oz) butter

Scrape the carrots, cut to an even size and boil them in salted water for about 20 minutes. Rinse them in cold water, and drain off any excess water. Heat the sugar gently in a frying pan until it is light brown, then add the butter. Turn the carrots in the caramel until they are golden brown.

Serve with a bacon joint or with slices of ham, peas and buttered potatoes.   *Serves 4.*

Red Cabbage
Rødkål

Red cabbage is an extremely popular and colourful vegetable. It is in season from October to February and even in the summer pickled red cabbage remains in favour as an accompaniment to cold pork and *frikadeller*.

1 medium-sized red cabbage, about 1kg (2lb) in weight	150ml (¼ pint) water salt
2 cooking apples	30–60ml (2–4 tbsp)
50g (2oz) butter	red- or blackcurrant
150ml (¼ pint) white wine vinegar	juice or jelly 40g (1½oz) sugar

Clean the cabbage, removing the outer leaves and stalks. Slice it fairly finely. Mix it with the peeled and sliced apple and put it in the melted butter with the vinegar and water. Cook for about 1½ hours or until very tender. Season with a little salt and stir in the red- or blackcurrant juice or jelly, and the sugar. Taste and adjust seasoning. The flavour should be both sweet and sour. *Serves 6–8.*

Spinach in Sauce
Stuvet spinat

40g (1½oz) butter	salt and pepper
40g (1½oz) flour	pinch sugar
400ml (¾ pint) milk	1kg (2lb) fresh spinach

Melt the butter in a pan and stir in the flour. Remove from the heat and gradually add the milk, stirring constantly. Bring to the boil and cook for 4–5 minutes, stirring, until fairly thick. Season to taste and keep hot.

Wash and drain the spinach and put it through a mincer. Mix it into the sauce and cook 2–3 minutes. This is a splendid way to capture the full flavour of spinach. Curly kale is also cooked in this way. *Serves 4.*

Peas and Carrots in Sauce
Stuvede grønærter og gulerødder

250g (8oz) peas	15g (½oz) butter
250g (8oz) carrots	15g (½oz) flour

Cook the vegetables until tender in approximately 150ml (¼ pint) water to which a little salt is added. Work the butter and flour together to form a ball and, when vegetables are cooked, thicken the cooking water by stirring in pieces of the flour ball until a sauce is formed. Alternatively, the vegetables may be drained, and the butter and flour mixed in the saucepan over a gentle heat and the vegetable stock slowly added. When thickened, return vegetables to sauce. Serve with hamburgers or *frikadeller*. This is also good with a little chopped ham added, served in *tarteletter* cases (page 21). *Serves 4.*

Buttered Cabbage
Smørdampet kål

500g (1lb) spring cabbage, savoy cabbage, or summer cabbage	salt 50g (2oz) butter

Wash and cut the cabbage in the usual way. Boil it in slightly salted water until partly cooked, about 10 minutes. Drain the cabbage well. Melt the butter in a non-stick pan, add the half-cooked cabbage and let it simmer in the butter with a lid on until tender, approximately 10 minutes. *Serves 4.*

Hot Potato Salad
Varm kartoffelsalat

750g (1½lb) new potatoes
50g (2oz) onion
40g (1½oz) butter
200ml (7fl oz) water or
   stock
15ml (1 tbsp) wine
   vinegar

pinch sugar
pinch salt
pinch pepper
chives or parsley to
   garnish

Boil the potatoes in their skins, then peel and slice them. Cut the onion thinly and fry until translucent in the butter. Add the water and simmer for 3–4 minutes. Then add vinegar and seasonings. Put the potatoes into this sauce, taking care not to break them. Reheat and serve garnished with chopped chives or parsley. A little milk or cream added to the salad gives the potatoes a good sheen.

This is nice with Frankfurter sausages which can be heated through while the salad is being made, or with *frikadeller*. *Serves 4.*

Chef's Salad
Salat med skinke og Danablu

½ cos lettuce
1 bunch radishes
5-cm (2-in) piece
   cucumber
1 onion
225g (8oz) cooked ham
125g (4oz) Danish Blue
   cheese

pinch salt
pinch pepper
pinch dry mustard
pinch caster sugar
60ml (4 tbsp) oil
30ml (2 tbsp) wine
   vinegar

Wash and cut lettuce and radishes. Slice cucumber, skin and finely slice the onion and separate it into rings. Cut ham into fairly thick strips. Cut the Danish Blue cheese into small cubes. Arrange these ingredients in alternate layers in a glass bowl. Place the seasonings in a bowl, blend with the oil, gradually beat in the vinegar and pour mixture over the salad. *Serves 3–4.*

Gypsy Salad, Salad in Tomatoes and (in bowl) Havarti Cheese Salad (page 70)

Gypsy Salad
Kartoffelsalat med Havarti og spegepølse

125g (4oz) Havarti cheese	125g (4oz) mayonnaise
125g (4oz) salami or cervelat sausage	2.5ml (½ tsp) mustard
	2.5ml (½ tsp) salt
50g (2oz) cooked, peeled potatoes	2.5ml (½ tsp) paprika
	50g (2oz) cooked peas
¼ cucumber	

Cut the cheese and sausage into cubes. Slice the potatoes. Dice the cucumber. Season the mayonnaise with the mustard, salt and paprika and fold in the peas and other ingredients. Place them in a bowl and garnish with a little lettuce and a sprig of dill or fennel. *Serves 3–4.* (Illustration page 69.)

Salad in Tomatoes
Tomater med oste- og skinkefyld

125g (4oz) Havarti cheese	salt
50g (2oz) ham	pepper
3 large salad tomatoes	mustard
oil	½ lettuce
vinegar	chives

Cut the cheese and ham neatly into small pieces. Cut the tops off the tomatoes and hollow them out. Make a piquant salad dressing with the oil, vinegar and seasonings. Pour this over the cheese and ham. Fill the tomatoes and serve on lettuce garnished with sprigs of chives. (Illustration page 69.)

Havarti Cheese Salad in Marinade   **Havarti og grønsagssalat**

125g (4oz) Havarti cheese	90ml (6 tbsp) salad oil
1 lettuce	2.5ml (½ tsp) mustard
¼ cucumber	5ml (1 tsp) sugar
3 tomatoes	30ml (2 tbsp) vinegar
125g (4oz) cauliflower	

Cut the cheese into thin strips. Wash and dry the lettuce. Slice the cucumber and tomatoes. Wash and dry the cauliflower and break it into small florets. Mix the remaining ingredients for a marinade, shaking it well. Arrange the cheese and salad vegetables in a glass bowl and dress with the marinade before serving. *Serves 3–4.* (Illustration page 69.)

Cold Potato Salad
Kold kartoffelsalat

1kg (2lb) firm potatoes	5ml (1 tsp) salt
300ml (½ pint) plain yoghurt	5ml (1 tsp) curry powder little lemon juice
45ml (3 tbsp) mayonnaise	tomatoes and cress
30ml (2 tbsp) chopped onion	

Scrub the potatoes and boil them gently in their skins in salt water. Drain and peel them. When cold, cut into thin slices.

Mix yoghurt and mayonnaise. Season with onion, salt, curry powder and lemon juice. Add potatoes into the dressing and decorate the salad with tomatoes and cress.

The potato salad can be served with various meat and fish dishes, like *frikadeller* or fried fillet of plaice. *Serves 4–6.*

Danish Blue Salad Dressing
Danablu dressing

150ml (¼ pint) olive oil	5ml (1 tsp) paprika
150ml (¼ pint) lemon juice	50g (2oz) Danish Blue cheese, grated
15ml (1 tbsp) sugar	
5ml (1 tsp) salt	

Using a large screw-top jar, shake all the ingredients together thoroughly and chill. Use as a salad dressing with lettuce, chicory or endive.

Cucumber Salad
Agurkesalat

This inexpensive salad is delicious with fried chicken or pork chops and is a common garnish on *smørrebrød* especially with chicken or *frikadeller*.

1 cucumber	*45ml (3 tbsp) water*
10ml (2 tsp) salt	*75g (3oz) sugar*
45ml (3 tbsp) white wine	*2.5ml ($\frac{1}{2}$ tsp) pepper*
* vinegar*	

Wash the cucumber and slice it very thinly without removing the skin. Put the slices into a bowl and mix with the salt. Leave until the juices have been released.

Squeeze well with the hand or between two saucers to remove moisture and put the cucumber into a fresh bowl. Pour the dressing, made from vinegar, water, sugar and pepper, over the cucumber. Mix well and leave the salad to chill before serving. *Serves 4–6.*

Pickled Beetroot
Syltede rødbeder

It is so simple to prepare pickled beetroot at home that it seems a shame to spend money on buying it. It keeps for 2–3 weeks in a larder and even longer in the refrigerator.

500g (1lb) beetroots	*50g (2oz) sugar*
300ml ($\frac{1}{2}$ pint) wine	*few strips of fresh*
* vinegar*	* horseradish*
150ml ($\frac{1}{4}$ pint) water	

Wash the beetroots but do not peel them. Cook them in water until tender, about 1$\frac{1}{2}$–2 hours. Allow to cool, then peel and slice them. Pack the slices into screw-top glass jars. Bring vinegar, water, sugar and horseradish to the boil and pour over the beets until they are completely covered. The beetroot should taste slightly sweet and sour. Cover the jars for storage. *Makes 500g (1lb).*

Rhubarb Compote
Rabarberkompot

Why not try the traditional Danish way of enjoying a pot-roasted young chicken, browned to a turn in butter (page 44), and served with butter-browned and plain potatoes and this rhubarb compote.

500g (1lb) rhubarb	*300ml ($\frac{1}{2}$ pint) water*
100g (4oz) sugar	

Cut the rhubarb into neat sticks about 2.5cm (1in) long. Boil the sugar with the water until dissolved. Add the rhubarb and bring slowly to boiling point again (do not let it over cook at this stage). Remove pan from heat but leave rhubarb in the saucepan with the lid on for a further 15 minutes. Remove the rhubarb with a slotted spoon and place it in a glass bowl.

Bring the juice to the boil again without covering the pan and reduce it by half. Pour this syrup over the rhubarb pieces. Cool and serve with meat dishes, especially chicken.

Butter Sauces and Garnishes

If you like your food to be simple but good then you are probably already a dedicated butter cook. It is an entirely natural food that gives a classic touch to ordinary meals and has a flavour that improves the enjoyment of everything with which it is served.

Danish cooks use a lactic-type butter, that is to say butter made from cream to which a culture is added to develop the flavour, rather in the way milk is treated to make yoghurt. It can be either slightly salted or unsalted and is exported under the name of Lurpak.

Denmark also produces a yellow, sweet-cream salted butter called Danelea. Generally speaking people in northern Britain prefer Lurpak, as they do in Denmark, while southerners like Danelea. It's all a matter of taste.

In making butter sauces the use of slightly salted or unsalted butter is recommended.

Hollandaise Sauce

Hollandaisesauce

30ml (2 tbsp) water	*100g (4oz) butter*
10ml (2 tsp) white wine	*2 large egg yolks*
vinegar	*salt*
6 peppercorns	*pepper*
blade of mace	*lemon juice*

Place the water, vinegar, peppercorns and mace in a small saucepan. Heat gently and reduce to 15ml (1 tbsp). Strain and allow to cool. Put the butter in a small saucepan and heat gently to *just* melt. Allow to cool.

Place the egg yolks, salt and cooled vinegar in a small bowl over a pan of cold water, heat very gently whisking the egg yolks until they are thick and pale. Remove bowl from the heat, gradually whisk in the melted butter, add extra salt, pepper and lemon juice if a sharper flavour is liked. Serve warm with fish, steaks, broccoli spears.

Béarnaise Sauce

Bearnaisesauce

30ml (2 tbsp) tarragon	*75g (3oz) butter, very soft*
vinegar	*5ml (1 tsp) chopped*
15ml (1 tbsp) water	*tarragon*
10ml (2 tsp) chopped	*5ml (1 tsp) chopped*
onion	*chervil (if available)*
2 egg yolks	*pepper*
pinch salt	

Place the vinegar, water and onion in a small saucepan. Reduce to 15ml (1 tbsp), strain and allow to cool.

Place the egg yolks, salt and cooled vinegar in a small bowl over a pan of cold water and heat very gently, whisking the egg yolks until they are thick and pale. Remove bowl from the heat.

Gradually whisk in the soft butter. If the sauce becomes too thick return bowl to the saucepan to heat gently. Stir in the herbs, pepper, taste and adjust seasonings. Serve warm.

Whipped Butter Sauce

Rørt smør

In this sauce the butter is simply whipped until light and fluffy but not melted, then piled into a small bowl and set on the table. Whipped butter sauce is spooned over plain boiled vegetables or in some cases over meat or fish, and served with soufflés. It is particularly good with artichokes.

100g (4 oz) butter

Take the butter out of the refrigerator and allow it to come to room temperature. Put it in a mixing bowl and cream it, using the back of a metal spoon which should be dipped occasionally in warm water. When the butter is light and peaky and has taken up a little of the water, it is ready to serve.

You can vary the flavour and make a green butter by adding 2.5ml ($\frac{1}{2}$ tsp) chopped parsley, dill, or tarragon leaves. Chopped garlic and horseradish are also good.

Melted Butter Sauce

Smeltet smør

Even quicker to serve than Whipped Butter Sauce is melted butter. There is no need to reserve this delicious sauce for asparagus. It is excellent with fish, steaks and vegetables. Just melt 100g (4oz) butter in a pan without browning and transfer it to a heated sauceboat. Stir in 30ml (2 tbsp) cold water to thicken the sauce just before serving.

Brown Butter Sauce

Brunet smør

Melt 50g (2oz) butter gently in a pan until golden brown. Add 30ml (2 tbsp) chopped parsley. Pour the sauce over boiled new potatoes and serve at once.

Caviar Butter

Kaviarsmør

Cream 50g (2oz) butter, preferably unsalted. Using a fork, gently add 10ml (2 tsp) mock caviar. Form the butter into a roll, wrap in greaseproof paper and place in the refrigerator until required. Serve in slices with fried or steamed fish.

Butter with Herbs and Spices

Urtesmør

At holiday times or when a lot of entertaining is in the air, these flavoured butters can be made up and stored in the refrigerator for about 1 week. It is important, though, to use freshly purchased butter, and any herbs should be thoroughly washed and dried.

Cream 100g (4oz) butter in a bowl until it is the consistency of stiffly whipped cream. Then add finely chopped herbs or the seasoning as suggested here. When dried herbs are used, use only half the stated quantity. Put the mixture in greaseproof paper and roll it into an even sausage shape about 2.5cm (1in) in diameter. Wrap again in foil and put the butter in the refrigerator to firm. Use knobs of herb butters when cooking vegetables, or cut in slices as a garnish to cooked dishes. Alternatively, the butter can be put in little pots for guests to spread on rolls or crispbread with soup or cheese. A fine touch to the dinner table!

Parsley Butter Add 5ml (1 tsp) lemon juice and 15ml (1 tbsp) chopped parsley. Serve with fried or grilled fish.

Mint Butter Add 15ml (1 tbsp) freshly chopped mint. Serve with lamb dishes or with plain omelettes.

Rosemary Butter Pick a sprig of fresh rosemary. Strip the spiky leaves off the stem and cut them finely before adding to the butter. Good with boiled spaghetti and macaroni.

Chive Butter Add 15ml (1 tbsp) finely chopped fresh chives. Serve with jacket potatoes or grilled meats.

Curry Butter Add 1.25–2.5ml ($\frac{1}{4}$–$\frac{1}{2}$ tsp) curry powder, depending on taste, and a pinch of ginger and cayenne pepper. Serve with plain boiled rice or on steaks.

Cinnamon Butter Do not cream the butter, but cut it into 15-g ($\frac{1}{2}$-oz) square pieces. Put a little powdered cinnamon on a saucer (curry and paprika are also good used this way) and dip the butter squares in the spice, turning to coat on all sides. Cinnamon butter goes well with rice pudding.

Storing Butter Butter should be stored in a cool place, preferably a refrigerator. Keep it wrapped, as light reduces the vitamin D content. Buy weekly for maximum flavour but if longer storage becomes necessary it will keep for 1 month in the refrigerator. In the freezer sweet-cream butter does not keep as long as lactic butters. Freezer storage times are: Danelea, salted sweet-cream butter, 2 months; Lurpak, slightly salted, lactic butter, 4 months; Lurpak, unsalted, lactic butter, 6 months.

Cold Butter

Koldt smør

It is quite common to hear a Dane talk of a certain dish being served with 'cold butter', which shows how well aware the speaker is of the possibility of serving butter in other delightful ways. Butter served straight from the refrigerator, firm and cool is the finest and simplest of all sauces with vegetables, meat and fish. It needs no preparation or further seasoning unless you wish it. And it is the spread *par excellence* for bread.

Cheeses of Denmark

People all over the world enjoy cheese and the Danes are no exception, but what a surprise on one's first morning in Denmark to find slices of it on the breakfast table! And as the day goes by their fondness for cheese becomes even more apparent. Cheese usually pops up again at midday on *smørrebrød* and often later for a little late-night snack. They are among the top cheese-lovers of the world, eating more than the British and Americans and only slightly less than the French.

Visitors quickly notice the small cheese slicers or a type of cutter with a thin wire on the cheese board. These are used to slice the traditional Danish cheeses like Samsoe and Danbo which are rather soft and yielding compared to Cheddar, and do not crumble or break when cut.

Shoppers often taste cheese before buying it freshly cut, because they buy quite large pieces at a time and naturally they do not want to be disappointed with the flavour.

Denmark is one of the biggest exporters of cheese in the world and the success of Danish Blue cheese has been a triumph for the skill of Danish cheese-makers. Originally it was made as a substitute for imported Roquefort, sadly missed by the cheese-loving Danes in the First World War. Now it is a cheese in its own right and recognized by cheese authorities everywhere by its official name of Danablu. This success has encouraged Danish cheese-makers to copy the cheeses of many lands and Danish Cheddar, a top prize-winner at many international cheese shows, is another more recent success.

1 Samsoe	6 Havarti	11 Maribo
2 Svenbo	7 Danish Blue	12 Esrom
3 Danbo with caraway	8 Havarti	13 Danish Cheddar
4 Mycella	9 Samsoe	14 Danish Blue
5 Mini-Havarti	10 Mycella	

Guide to Danish Cheeses
Vejledning om danske oste

SAMSOE   This is Denmark's national cheese and is the one that most resembles Cheddar in flavour. It is a semi-firm cheese with a few holes or 'eyes', golden yellow in colour and takes its name from the island of Samsoe off the east Jutland coast. Good for sandwiches or the cheese board, melts easily in cooking, can be used cubed or grated, and is easy to slice.

DANBO Similar to Samsoe but often paler in colour and slightly softer. May be protected by a red or yellow coloured wax over the rind. It is a popular breakfast cheese in Denmark. The caraway flavoured version is used on the cheese board and for *smørrebrød*.

TYBO A rectangular, loaf-shaped cheese also belonging to the Samsoe group of cheeses. It often has a red or yellow wax coating. Tybo has a number of regularly shaped pea-sized holes, and is a nice mild cheese much enjoyed by children. Is sometimes flavoured with caraway seeds.

ELBO Similar to Tybo but rather firmer. Nice and mild.

FYNBO A round yellow cheese with a number of holes rather like Samsoe. Takes its name from the island of Funen, the garden of Denmark. When cut it is yielding, yet close in texture. Mild in flavour.

MOLBO A comfortable ball-shaped cheese with a red wax coating. Rather yellow in colour with a few round holes. Exceptionally mild.

MARIBO A firm-textured cheese, easy to slice and with a fuller flavour than the Samsoe-type cheeses listed above. Has numerous irregular holes, small and rather close together. A speciality of excellent quality.

HAVARTI A cheese of character with a good, clean aromatic flavour. Yellow with numerous holes both big and little. A nice choice after dinner and excellent in salads.

ESROM This is a piquant cheese, thin rinded with numerous holes. The flavour is mild yet subtle, and slightly aromatic. Sometimes known as Danish Port Salut or by the brand name of the various cheese dairies where it is made.

DANABLU Danish Blue is the original Danablu cheese. Blue veins on a white ground are its distinguishing features. It has a pleasantly sharp, piquant flavour. Immensely useful as an after-dinner cheese with a glass of wine or at midday with ice-cold lager, and gives an intriguing flavour to many cooked dishes.

MYCELLA The creamy yellow colour and evenly distributed green veins distinguish Mycella on sight from Danablu. The taste is smooth, mellow and piquant. This is a cheese for the connoisseur and only a limited quantity is exported.

DANISH CHEDDAR A cheese with the clean, well-flavoured Cheddar taste and crumbly texture. Both white Cheddar and red Cheddar are made.

SVENBO A semi-hard but sliceable cheese with a characteristic sweetish flavour. There are large distinctive holes about 1cm ($\frac{1}{4}$in) to 2.5cm (1in) in diameter.

DANISH EMMENTALER A hard dry cheese marked with large holes which often run into each other. Outstanding as a table cheese and in cooked dishes.

DANISH ST PAULIN Yellowish, compact with a few small round holes. Piquant flavour.

DANISH FONTINA Also called Fontal. A soft sweetish cheese that occasionally has small round holes.

DANISH GRANA A dry firm cheese with a hard black or greyish rind. Rather sweet and piquant. An excellent flavoured cheese for cooking.

DANISH MOZZARELLA White, rindless. Mild flavour. Used for cooking, especially with pizzas.

DANISH CAMEMBERT Has a white crust which can be eaten. Before the cheese matures it has a firm whitish centre turning to pale yellow as it ripens. The flavour is regarded as mushroom-like.

DANISH BRIE A mild, aromatic pale yellow to white cheese with a soft white edible rind.

DANISH FETA A white fresh cheese in brine. Salty, piquant flavour. Nice in salads.

DANISH WHITE MOULD CHEESE (or full fat soft cheese) Several varieties are produced with or without blue veining. These cheeses are rather similar to Brie in flavour and in their creamy, soft texture. In the blue-veined varieties, the Brie flavour is deliciously combined with the taste of the blue-veining.

DANISH CREAM CHEESES AND SPREADS Soft and easy to spread. Plain, smoked or with various flavours: herbs, liqueurs, fruits, shrimps, ham, mushroom, etc. Producing dairies use their own brand name.

Cheese Dips
Ostedip

The dipping idea is an old Danish custom. At mealtimes on the farms in the really old days, the farmer's wife set the porridge bowl in the centre of the table and everyone ate from the same bowl. Each 'dipper', however, had his own spoon which he wiped on his sleeve when he finished eating before hanging it in the spoon rack ready for the next meal. Compared with this custom, the twentieth-century cheese dip is certainly more hygienic, with biscuits or raw vegetables provided to spoon up the food.

Creamy Mycella Dip

Mix together 100g (4oz) Mycella cheese with 50g (2oz) Danish cream cheese. Add just sufficient milk to give the mixture the consistency of very thick cream. Serve garnished with chives.

Celery Dip

225g (8oz) Danish Blue cheese
10ml (2 tsp) grated onion
2 sticks celery finely chopped
60ml (4 tbsp) milk

Break up the Danish Blue cheese with a fork, add the remaining ingredients, and mix well together until fairly soft, adding more milk if necessary. Place in a glass and decorate with a few celery leaves. Serve with celery sticks cut in pieces or sprigs of raw cauliflower, pieces of carrot and potato crisps.

Danbo Dip

100g (4oz) Danbo cheese (without caraway)
50g (2oz) Danish cream cheese
45ml (3 tbsp) tomato ketchup
75ml (5 tbsp) milk
30ml (2 tbsp) chopped red pimentos
15ml (1 tbsp) chopped green pimentos
few drops Worcestershire sauce

Grate the Danbo cheese and stir it into the cream cheese. Stir in remaining ingredients. Spoon mixture into a serving bowl and leave in a cool place for 1 hour before serving to blend the flavours.

Blue Cheese and Avocado Dip

100g (4oz) Danish Blue cheese
150ml ($\frac{1}{4}$ pint) soured cream
50g (2oz) chopped walnuts
1 avocado pear
15ml (1 tbsp) lemon juice
pepper

Crumble the cheese and mash it with a fork. Stir in the soured cream and walnuts. Halve the avocado, remove stone and skin. Mash the flesh with the lemon juice. Add the cheese, mix well and season with pepper.

This dip should be made no more than an hour before needed. Keep covered and stir before serving.

Cheese for a Special Occasion Ost til festlige lejligheder

There is a most distinctive style to a Danish party cheese board. Great importance is attached to offering a cheese to suit everyone's taste – some mild yellow cheeses like Samsoe or Havarti, one or two veined cheeses like Danish Blue or Mycella, or the newer blue-veined white mould cheeses. And more often than not a little Brie or Camembert. All the cheeses will be partly cut and neatly displayed on the board, making it easy to help yourself.

The fruit, vegetables or nuts which often accompany these boards are listed here against the cheese types.

Danbo   Celery, pineapple, cherries
Danish Blue   Black grapes, walnuts
Danish Brie   Tangerines, grapes
Danish Camembert   Mandarin oranges or red pepper
Danish Emmentaler   Pears, walnuts
Elbo   Apples, pears, bananas
Esrom   Celery, tomatoes, walnuts, watercress
Fynbo   Cucumber, spring onions, tomato wedges
Havarti   Tomatoes, cucumber, celery, olives
Maribo   Radishes, tomatoes, green pepper, celery
Molbo   Radishes, green pepper
Mycella   Green grapes, fresh strawberries
Samsoe   Tomatoes, apples, bananas, mixed nuts
Tybo   Tomato, apples

Cheese Buffet for Twelve

Osteanretning til 12 personer

When friends come for a drink and a talk, a cheese tray is something you can serve with tea or coffee, wine or a glass of *snaps*.

Use a nice clean plank of plain wood for this cheese board. It sets the cheeses off beautifully and will make a little talking point at the party. The quantities given are approximate.

375g (13oz) Danbo or Samsoe cheese	*750g (1½lb) Danish Brie*
375g (13oz) Tybo or Danbo with caraway seeds	*300g (11oz) Danish Camembert*
500g (1lb) mini-Havarti cheese	*radishes, walnuts, grapes, cucumber, green and red peppers to garnish*
500g (1lb) Danish Blue cheese	

Cut and slice the cheeses as shown and arrange on the board with the garnishes. Serve with bread, biscuits and butter.

1 Mini-Havarti (piece and slices)
2 Danish Camembert
3 Tybo with caraway
4 Grapes
5 Danish Blue Cheese
6 Danish Blue Cheese with walnuts
7 Danbo
8 Radishes
9 Danish Brie
10 Tybo with caraway
11 Danish Camembert
12 Cucumber
13 Danbo
14 Green and red peppers

Samsoe Sputnik

Samsø-Sputnik

Let the children make this for a tea-time treat. They will love both preparing and eating it.

Cut 175g (6oz) Samsoe cheese into cubes. Cut a slice from one end of an orange to make a firm base. Pierce the cheese cubes with cocktail sticks. Add a grape, cherry, mandarin segment or piece of pineapple to each cube. Push the other end of the cocktail stick into the orange to form a decorated 'sputnik'.

Samsoe Shrimpy (page 82), Samsoe Sputnik, and Samsoe Danwich

Samsoe Shrimpy

Gyldent reje- og ostebrød

This is a good supper dish, or can be served as a starter.

75g (3oz) Samsoe cheese	salt and pepper
175g (6oz) shrimps	40g (1½oz) butter
30ml (2 tbsp) mayonnaise	4 slices white bread
15ml 1 tbsp) soured cream or yoghurt	2 egg whites parsley sprig
juice of ¼ lemon	

Grate the Samsoe cheese. Reserving some shrimps for the garnish, mix the remainder with the mayonnaise, soured cream or yoghurt, and lemon juice. Season with salt and pepper. Butter the bread and place the shrimp mixture on it. Whisk egg whites until stiff and fold in the grated Samsoe cheese. Spread this mixture on the bread, covering the shrimps and mayonnaise. Cook for 20–25 minutes at 200°C(400°F)/Gas 6 until golden brown. Garnish with remaining shrimps and a sprig of parsley. *Serves 2.*

Mycella Party Pieces

Mycella selskabsbidder

Mycella is a lovely cheese to serve at a dinner party. Its natural affinity with wine makes it a memorable finish to a meal. But it is also good for *smørrebrød*, snacks, and cocktail tit-bits. (Illustration pages 2 and 3.)

Open Sandwiches Arrange a slice of Mycella cheese on well-buttered rye bread. Garnish it with strawberries in summertime or glacé cherries, tomatoes, etc., in other seasons.

Mycella Snacks Butter fingers or squares of bread and top the slices with creamy Mycella cheese. Decorate with sliced olives or radishes. A satisfying tit-bit.

Cocktail Cubes Cut Mycella cheese neatly into 2.5-cm (1-in) cubes. Using cocktail sticks, secure a grape, mandarin orange segment or an olive to each cube. Sandwich some of the cubes between two walnut halves. Pretty, and irresistible for parties.

Danish Cheese Fondue

Dansk ostefondue

It is important to have the table laid and the bread ready, cut either in slices or cubes, before making the fondue which must be served at once.

1–2 cloves garlic	30ml (1 tbsp) snaps or kirsch
350g (12 oz) grated Danish Emmentaler	pinch bicarbonate of soda
350g (12oz) grated Samsoe	salt and pepper pinch grated nutmeg
15ml (1 tbsp) cornflour	French bread, cubed
450ml (¾ pint) dry white wine	

Peel and halve the garlic and rub round the sides and bottom of a fondue pot, leaving the cloves in the bottom. Add the grated cheeses, cornflour and white wine, bring gently to the boil over a medium heat, stirring continuously in a figure of eight for about 5 minutes to melt the cheese. Mix the *snaps* or *kirsch* and bicarbonate of soda together and add to the pot. Stir, adding the seasonings to taste, and place over fondue burner at once.

The fondue should be kept warm and eaten with small pieces of bread on a fondue fork gently stirred into the fondue to lightly coat. Try to keep the fondue moving, as it will gradually thicken. *Serves 4.*

Fried Danish Camembert

Friturestegt dansk Camembert

2 portions Danish Camembert	fat for deep frying French bread
1 egg	blackcurrant jam
breadcrumbs	

Turn the cheese in beaten egg and then in breadcrumbs. The surface must be completely covered with the breadcrumbs. Heat the oil, and deep fry the cheese until light brown and crisp.

Serve as a dessert after the main course with blackcurrant jam and toast. *Serves 2.*

Cheese Layer Cake
Ostelagkage

6 50-g (2-oz) portions
    Danish Camembert
100g (4oz) Danish cream
    cheese
15ml (1 tbsp) dry sherry

30ml (2 tbsp) coarsely
    chopped almonds
30ml (2 tbsp) sliced
    grapes
almonds and grapes to
    garnish

With a sharp knife, cut the cheese portions in half lengthwise, forming two layers. In a small bowl, blend the cream cheese with sherry to soften, then add almonds and grapes. Reserve 15ml (1 tbsp) for garnish and spread remainder on the bottom layer of the cheese. Carefully place the top layer on the filling. Assemble the portions in a circle. Garnish with the reserved cream cheese mixture and add a few more almonds and grapes on top. Serve on the buffet table or on the cheese board.

Cheese Medals
Ostemedailler

BISCUITS:
150g (5oz) butter
yolk of 1 large egg

225g (8oz) flour, sifted
salt, pepper, mustard

FILLING:
75g (3oz) butter
150g (6oz) Danish Blue
    cheese, crumbled

salt and pepper
approx. 30ml (2 tbsp)
    milk

Soften the butter with a wooden spoon and beat in the egg yolk. Blend in the flour and seasoning. Knead well. Wrap dough and put in a cool place for 1 hour.

Preheat the oven 200°C(400°F)/Gas 6. Roll out the dough on a floured board. Using a 2.5-cm (1-in) cutter, cut into rounds and place on a baking sheet. Cook for approximately 10 minutes until pale golden brown. Cool on a wire rack.

To make the filling, soften the butter and blend with crumbled cheese, season and add a little milk to make the mixture a soft consistency.

Sandwich the biscuits together with the filling and serve at coffee time or with the cheese board. *Makes about 24.*

Danish Blue Cheese Gâteau
Danablu ostekage

PASTRY:
225g (8oz) self-raising
    flour
salt

75g (3oz) butter
30ml (2 tbsp) mayonnaise
60–75ml (4–5 tbsp) milk

FILLING:
175g (6oz) Danish Blue
    cheese
150ml ($\frac{1}{4}$ pint) double
    cream
50g (2oz) celery
pepper

225g (8oz) tomatoes
50g (2oz) cream
    cheese
celery leaves for garnish

Preheat oven to 200°C(400°F)/Gas 6. Sieve the flour with a pinch of salt and rub in the butter. Add the mayonnaise and enough milk to make a pliable dough. Divide in 2. Knead each piece, and roll out and trim one round using a 21.5-cm (8½-in) plate as a guide. Place on a baking sheet. Roll remaining pastry to same size, place on second baking sheet and divide into 8 triangles. Bake for 15 minutes, then leave the pastry to cool on the baking sheets.

Mash Danish Blue cheese with a fork. Beat the cream until just softly stiff and stir two-thirds of it into the cheese. Finely chop the celery, add to the cheese with a little pepper and mix well.

Place the circle of pastry on a flat plate, slice the tomatoes fairly thinly and arrange them on the pastry, keeping back 4 pieces for decoration. Spread the mixture over the tomatoes. Place the triangles of pastry on top of the cheese. Mix the cream cheese and remaining cream together. Place it in a piping bag and pipe a large rosette on each triangle of pastry. Decorate rosettes with celery leaves and the reserved tomato.

Ideal as a savoury at the end of a meal, or to serve at a cheese and wine party. *Serves 8.*

Overleaf – Smørrebrød – foreground, left to right:
Samsoe cheese with lettuce, radish and parsley; cod's roe with rémoulade sauce; marinated herrings with onion rings; Danish ham with Russian salad; Danish salami with onion rings; liverpâté with fried mushrooms and bacon; hard-boiled egg with mayonnaise, caviar and lemon; (centre) ham with sliced scrambled egg
background – in addition may be seen:
Danish Blue cheese with grapes; hard-boiled egg with mayonnaise and Danish bacon

Smørrebrød (Open Sandwiches)

Once you become acquainted with *smørrebrød* – Danish open sandwiches – you will find them a great culinary experience and great fun to serve. Making them is a unique field of cookery – a cross, perhaps, between sandwiches and salads, but with no real comparison with either as we know them. *Smørrebrød* is a small meal in its own right – containing the meats, fish and vegetables (or, indeed, cheese) of your choice but with bread instead of potatoes and with good butter as the 'sauce'. That is the way to think of *smørrebrød* as you come to make them – each a complete little dish on its own.

When you plan an entire meal of *smørrebrød*, take the normal composition of a meal into account and make it a two-, three- or four-course 'menu' according to appetite and occasion. Thus you might begin with fish, lightly garnished, continue with one or two meat 'dishes', each with a medley of vegetables or a fruit garnish, and go on to cheese. There are even a few sweet dessert *smørrebrød*, or you could serve a 'pudding' – mostly fruit salad in cream – but normally you would finish with coffee and a Danish pastry or a cream cake.

A really comprehensive selection of *smørrebrød* will include a number of freshly cooked toppings served lukewarm and put on the buttered bread at the last minute, or there may be fewer *smørrebrød* and a 'little warm dish' offered afterwards.

Snitter is the Danish word for half-sized *smørrebrød* made to eat in the fingers at cocktail parties and receptions. The toppings are the same as for ordinary *smørrebrød* but are used in small quantities and on smaller pieces of bread. Sometimes the food is made smaller still with cocktail sticks through the centre for easy handling. This is *pindemad* which means literally 'pin food'. They are a speciality of restaurants rather than the home.

Choosing the Bread

Danes use a dark rye bread for most kinds of *smørrebrød* but white or brown loaves, granary or French bread will work equally well as long as they are firm in texture and have a crisp crust.

The use of small pieces of bread is one of the distinguishing features of *smørrebrød*, and beginning with the right shape and size is a great help in achieving the correct appearance. Too large a base will spoil the compact effect. The bread should be cut approximately 5 × 10cm (2 × 4in) in size, i.e. about half a slice taken from a small tin loaf, and about 0.5cm ($\frac{1}{4}$in) thick.

Buttering it Right

The taste of well-made *smørrebrød* – clear and positive but without one taste overwhelming another – owes a great deal to the flavour of the good aromatic butter which Danes use on them. (Stop for a moment and try to think of any other spread for breads or biscuits which can be eaten on its own with such pleasure.) *Smørrebrød* actually means 'buttered bread' and the traditional Danish butter has the particular balance of creaminess and gentle saltiness which is ideal for them.

Smørrebrød need plenty of butter, and it should be spread right to the edge of the bread in one even smooth layer so that its flavour becomes a catalyst for all the other flavours. The butter serves a practical purpose, too, preventing the bread from becoming soggy with any moisture from the topping, and helping to hold everything in place.

How Much Topping

The quantity you use of the main ingredient can be as much or as little as your generosity, purse, taste or the occasion demands. Choose one main ingredient and make sure that it covers the bread entirely, putting a little lettuce leaf under it at one end if you want to give a lift to a particularly flat topping.

Garnishes

The garnish should be arranged with an eye to complementing the flavours and adding some colour. The following list will help in preparing any number of variations, but only one or two garnishes should be added to each piece. It is not intended that you should add them all or you will fall out with the purists in Denmark who constantly extol the virtues of *smørrebrød* with little garnish, like the ones children take to school.

Toppings

Beef, roast   Crisply fried onions, pickles, rémoulade sauce, grated horseradish.

Beef tartar   Onion ring, raw egg yolk, grated horseradish, capers, parsley.

CHEESES

Mild (Danbo, Samsoe, etc.)   Green pepper, radishes, celery, tomato.

Blue-veined (Danish Blue, Mycella, etc.) Black or green grapes, pears.

Danish Brie or Camembert   Mandarin segments, cress.

Strong (Havarti, Esrom)   Radishes, walnuts, tomato.

Chicken, roast Cucumber salad, lettuce, tomato, bacon rolls.

Duck, roast Prunes, pieces of lightly poached apple.

Eel, smoked   Scrambled egg strip, watercress.

Egg Lettuce and tomato, anchovies, mock caviar, mayonnaise, parsley, cress.

Ham Lettuce, egg, Italian salad, chopped green pepper, cucumber, tomato, parsley.

Herring (marinated, pickled, *gaffelbidder*, etc.)   Raw onion rings (or finely chopped onion), capers, snippets of tomato, cress, hard-boiled egg slices, parsley. Herrings taste best served on rye bread.

Liverpâté Crisply fried streaky bacon rasher, butter fried mushrooms, meat jelly, *asier* (pickled cucumbers), beetroot.

Mackerel, smoked Raw egg yolk, chopped hard-boiled egg, radishes, chives, cress.

Plaice, fried fillet   Lemon twists or quarters, rémoulade sauce, lettuce, cress.

Pork, roast   Red cabbage, prunes and apples, pickled cucumbers.

Potatoes Cold sliced new potatoes, mayonnaise, chives. Serve on rye or crisp bread.

Salami   Meat jelly and onion rings, parsley.

Salmon, smoked Lemon or dill, cress, strip of scrambled egg. Use white bread.

Sardines Lemon, sprig of fresh dill, sliced olives. Serve on rye or French bread.

Shrimps Mayonnaise, lemon, dill, cress or parsley, mock caviar, tomato snippets. Serve on French bread.

Tongue Lettuce, horseradish cream, Italian salad, sliced tomato, cress or parsley.

Service of 'Smørrebrød'

Wooden boards often serve as trays for *smørrebrød*. If you have not got one, a large plain-coloured platter of any shape will show them off just as well. Specially shaped servers, usually made of stainless steel, are used to lift them in Denmark. A palette knife or cake server can be used instead.

The most colourful way to arrange the *smørrebrød* is to put several kinds on the dish at once, taking care to keep any strong-smelling ones like herring and cheese away from more delicate flavours.

A knife and fork are needed to eat 'high-style' *smørrebrød*, and only one piece at a time should be taken on to your plate.

School Lunch

Danish children start school at 8.00 and take a box of *smørrebrød* to eat at lunchtime, around 11.00. These are plain and flat with little or no garnish. Most schools provide milk for the children, but there are no cooked meals.

Each piece is wrapped individually in greaseproof paper so that the flavours and toppings do not mingle, then packed into a plastic box or a tin. This flat style of *smørrebrød* is meant to be eaten with your fingers.

A typical school lunch-box would contain the following open sandwiches: 1 liverpâté and beetroot; 1 sliced, cold *frikadelle* with red cabbage; 1 or 2 salami, no garnish; 1 Danbo cheese, no garnish; 1 chocolate (on special occasions); and some fruit, such as an apple, orange or banana.

Office Lunch

Similar packets of *smørrebrød* are taken from home or bought from special sandwich shops on the way by office workers, or may be carried out to the fields by farm workers when they are very busy in spring or at harvest time.

As the topping for lunch-box *smørrebrød* is always modest, a typical selection for a man will be, say, 6 half-slices of bread with toppings of marinated herring and raw onion rings, liverpâté with parsley and cucumber, sliced hard-boiled egg with a slice of tomato and some cress, sliced tomato sprinkled with chopped chives, salami slices (plain or with meat jelly), and Samsoe or Danbo cheese.

Warm 'Smørrebrød'

It is quite usual for one piece of *smørrebrød* to be served hot, especially when the family are having lunch together. These are served on bread and butter in the same way as the cold *smørrebrød* and usually follow the herring and sausage sandwiches. Some hot *smørrebrød* are a slice of cooked ham with a freshly fried egg, freshly cooked lukewarm *frikadeller* with red cabbage, fillet of fish, usually plaice or sole, with rémoulade sauce, freshly fried liver topped with fried onions and streaky bacon, and thinly sliced pork tenderloin, freshly fried, with onions.

The Danwich

'Danwich' is the name given to Danish open sandwiches by the Danish Food Centres in Britain. It is easier to pronounce than *smørrebrød* and quicker to say than the vaguely inaccurate 'Danish open sandwich'. The word means quite simply an open sandwich made with authentic Danish ingredients.

Danwiches are the equivalent of the high style of *smørrebrød* served at parties and in restaurants.

Shrimp Crush
Rejer i trængsel (1)

lettuce	lemon slice
buttered white bread	tomato snippet
15g ($\frac{1}{2}$oz) mayonnaise	parsley sprig
25-50g (1-2oz) shrimps	

Press the lettuce leaf on to the butter in one corner of the bread. Spoon a little of the mayonnaise on to the other end, keeping some for decoration. Pile on the shrimps. Garnish with remaining mayonnaise, lemon, snippet of tomato and parsley sprig.

Variations: Arrange tomato slices on the bread, pipe on mayonnaise and garnish with a few shrimps.

Or use slices of hard-boiled egg next to the buttered bread topped with a little mayonnaise, shrimps and about 2.5ml ($\frac{1}{2}$ tsp) mock caviar for each Danwich. (Illustration page 88.)

Fried Fish Fillet
Stegt fiskefilet (2)

lettuce	lemon slice
buttered white bread	tomato
1 small piece fried fillet of plaice	parsley or cress
15ml (1 tbsp) rémoulade sauce	

Put the lettuce on the buttered bread with the lukewarm fillet of plaice on top. Garnish with rémoulade sauce, a lemon twist and a little tomato and cress.

Variation: The fish fillets may be cut into strips before cooking and 1 or 2 pieces used instead of whole fillets, when a more economical Danwich is needed. (Illustration page 88.)

88

7

8

9

10

Danwich Favourites

These attractive pictures illustrate the Danwich recipes on pages 87, 90 and 91 in a typically Danish style.

1 Shrimp Crush
2 Fried Fish Fillet
3 Herring with Onion
4 Roast Pork with Orange
5 Salami with Onion
6 Ham with Egg Strip
7 Liverpâté with Bacon
8 Sausage with Bacon
9 Bacon and Egg, Danish style
10 Blue Boy Danwich
11 Roast Beef Danwich

11

Herring Danwich
Et stykke med sild (3)

3 pieces herring: matjse, rollmop or marinated	3 onion rings
buttered rye or brown bread	parsley or cress
	tomato snippet

Arrange pieces of herring neatly on the buttered bread and decorate it with three graduated onion rings, a little parsley or cress, and a snippet of tomato just to add a touch of colour. This is one of the few Danwiches in which the buttered bread is expected to show.

Variations: Use 3 slices hard-boiled egg to cover one side of the bread and overlap the three pieces of herring on these. Decorate as before.

Or slice cold cooked new potatoes, arrange over the buttered bread, top with 1 or 2 pieces of herring and garnish thickly with finely chopped onion or chives. (Illustration page 88.)

Ham Danwich
Skinke (6)

1 slice canned ham or meat from a bacon joint	1 strip scrambled egg
buttered white or brown bread	2 slices cucumber
	slice tomato
	lettuce
	cress

Fold the meat on to the buttered bread. Cut an egg strip from scrambled egg, using slightly slanting cuts. Put this on the ham. Twist together the cucumber and the tomato slice and set down across the strip of egg. Decorate with a little lettuce and cress.

Variations: Italian salad with a slice of hard-boiled egg makes a decorative topping for ham. Finish with a single tomato and cucumber twist or other garnish as available. Potato salad or pineapple are also nice with ham. (Illustration page 88.)

Roast Beef Danwich
Roast beef (11)

1 or 2 slices roast beef	crisply fried onion
buttered bread	tomato snippet
rémoulade sauce	parsley or cress

A slice of beef is best laid flat on the bread, making sure it covers it neatly but not untidily, as it is usually too soft to fold to give height to the Danwich. Spoon on a little of the sauce and add the onion, grated horseradish and a piece of tomato and parsley.

Variations: Grated fresh horseradish can be added to the garnish or mild horseradish cream used to replace the rémoulade sauce. (Illustration page 89.)

Salami Danwich
Spegepølse (5)

3–4 slices salami	3 graduated onion rings
buttered rye or white bread	parsley

Fold the salami slices on to the bread as shown in the illustration to give the Danwich a little height and finish with the graduated onion rings and parsley. Danes advise you to eat the parsley as they claim it is not just there to make a touch of colour, but also takes away the smell of the onion from the breath.

Variations: Fold 3 slices salami on to the bread, put a slice of meat jelly on top, and sprinkle with chopped chives, or green tops of spring onion. (Illustration page 88.)

Blue Boy Danwich
Danablu (10)

lettuce	2 slices Danish Blue cheese
buttered bread	
1 walnut half	

Put the lettuce on the bread, add the slices of freshly cut Danish Blue and garnish with a half of walnut.

Variations: The cheese can be mashed with a fork, mixed with chopped onion, and then spread on the bread and garnished with a slice of tomato, and cress. A slice of red-skinned apple (dipped in lemon juice to prevent discolouring) or de-seeded black grapes can be used instead of the walnut. (Illustration page 89.)

Roast Pork
Flæskesteg (4)

rye or wholemeal buttered bread	crackling
1 slice roast pork	1 prune, cooked and stoned
little cold, cooked red cabbage	orange slice
	lettuce

Top the buttered bread with the meat, spoon on the red cabbage, add a tiny piece of cold crackling if available, the prune, a twist of orange, and a tiny piece of lettuce. Eat the Danwich pressing out the orange juice on to the meat with the knife or fork or pick up the whole slice and eat it in your fingers.

Variations: Any apples cooked around the meat can be used instead of the red cabbage, or a little apple sauce – so long as it is not too juicy. Slices of cooked pork can be bought at most delicatessen shops. (Illustration page 88.)

Bacon and Egg, Danish~style Bacon og æg (9)

lettuce (optional)	1 rasher crisply fried bacon
buttered bread	slice tomato
1 hard-boiled egg	cress

Put the lettuce on the bread, if you are using it, or arrange the slices of hard-boiled egg directly on top of the butter. Add a crisply fried rasher of bacon, tomato and some cress.

Variations: Use a piece of lukewarm grilled gammon steak or a bacon chop on the lettuce with slices of hard-boiled egg, tomato and the cress on top. (Illustration page 89.)

Liverpâté Danwich
Leverpostej (7)

lettuce	butter-fried mushrooms
buttered bread	gherkin
2 slices tinned or home-made liverpâté	tomato
1 piece crisply fried streaky bacon	

Put the lettuce on the bread and put two slices of liverpâté on top. If home-made pâté is used it can be roughly sliced or spread generously directly on to the bread. Add some bacon and mushrooms which can be either freshly cooked and lukewarm or cooked in advance and cold. Cut and fan out the gherkin before placing it on the Danwich. Finish with a piece of tomato.

Variations: A small finger of liverpâté is nice with a slice of tongue with a garnish of meat jelly, tomato and parsley. A sprinkling of crisply fried onions – the kind that come in packets – is a favourite with some people. (Illustration page 89.)

Sausage Danwich
Pølse (8)

lettuce	1 radish
buttered bread	1 piece crisply fried bacon
potato salad	
1 sausage	

Slip the lettuce on to the butter in one corner of the bread, heap on the potato salad, being as generous as you like, cut the sausage lengthwise (or it can be chopped in rings), place on the potato salad and decorate with the radish and a tasty piece of crispy bacon. This makes a delicious Danwich.

Variations: A little French mustard goes well on the sausage, and so do sweet pickles, gherkins, cocktail onions, fried onions or spring onions instead of radishes. But take care – only a few of these should be used on each Danwich. (Illustration page 89.)

A Danwich Party

There is plenty of fun to be had from giving a Danwich Party, and it is easy to do all the preparation well ahead. The *smørrebrød* will stay fresh for several hours if left in a cool place, lightly covered with cling film or damp greaseproof paper. Set them out on trays or flat dishes with knives, forks and small plates nearby. After the Danwiches serve a cheese tray and one or two typically Danish desserts, perhaps a sherry soufflé or strawberries and cream in season.

This Danwich Party menu for twelve allows two or three Danwiches for each person and is based on six kinds. Make six of each of the following:

Marinated herrings with raw onion or sliced hard-boiled egg.

Salami with onion rings or meat jelly.

Roast beef with rémoulade sauce, fried onions, tomato and cucumber twist.

Ham with egg strips, cucumber and tomato twist, lettuce and cress.

Liverpâté with bacon, gherkin, butter-fried mushrooms and tomato.

Potato salad with sausage, bacon, lettuce and radish or spring onion.

If you find it difficult to buy marinated herrings for the herring Danwich, rollmop herrings, sardines or anchovies all make good substitutes. Garnish sardines or anchovies with slices of hard-boiled egg and parsley instead of onion.

Danwich Shopping List for Party of Twelve

The list of ingredients given here is approximate as each person makes a Danwich slightly differently:

2–3 small loaves rye bread
225g (8oz) butter
18 slices Danish salami
1 jar of marinated herrings
6–12 slices roast beef, depending on size
6–12 slices of canned ham or cooked bacon joint
12 rashers streaky bacon
3 50-g (2-oz) cans Danish liverpâté
6 frankfurters
225g (8oz) potato salad
6 eggs
75g (3oz) rémoulade sauce
1 lettuce

6 tomatoes
small bunch parsley
fresh horseradish
1–2 onions, fried
1 punnet cress
125g (4oz) mushrooms, fried
5-cm (2-in) piece cucumber

Ham and Cheese Decker
Skinke- og ostesmørrebrød

3 thick slices bread
butter
2 lettuce leaves
2 thin slices cooked ham

50g (2oz) Danish Blue
cheese
1 tomato

Toast the bread on both sides and remove crusts. Butter the toast. Arrange lettuce on one slice and cover with the 2 pieces of ham folded into three and placed across the corners. Top with the second slice of toast. Slice the Danish Blue cheese and the tomato thinly and arrange on the toast. Cover with the third piece. Cut into two triangles and serve garnished with extra lettuce. Cold tongue is also nice in this sandwich.

A Little Night Food
Lidt natmad

This delicious toasted snack and the two following recipes would be perfect for the *natmad*, served just before guests leave a party with a last glass of lager and perhaps a glass of *snaps*

8 slices of streaky Danish
bacon
25g (1oz) butter
45ml (3 tbsp) flour
150ml ($\frac{1}{4}$ pint) milk or
cream

500g (1lb) mushrooms
salt
4–6 slices toasted French
bread

Cook the bacon until crisp. Melt the butter, stir in the flour and cook until it thickens, then stir in the milk or cream. Add the cleaned mushrooms and season with salt. Cook them just enough to get hot but not too soft. Arrange the creamed mushrooms on the buttered toast and place a slice or two of bacon on top. Serve at once. *Serves 4–6.*

Ham and Cheese Decker

Leeks with Bacon on Toast
Ristet brød med porrer og bacon

2–4 leeks	2–4 slices French bread
25–50g (1–2oz) butter	4 slices streaky bacon
salt	
50–100g (2–4oz) Danish	
Cheddar cheese, grated	

Wash the leeks, cut them into rings, and fry them gently until transparent in the butter. Sprinkle them with a little salt and add the grated cheese. Cook until the leeks are tender. Serve on toasted French bread with the crisply fried bacon on top.   *Serves 2–4.*

Crispy Ham Rolls
Sprøde rundstykker med skinkefyld

4 crisp round rolls	sandwich spread or
50g (2oz) butter	mayonnaise
100g (4oz) cooked ham	mustard
tomato	cress
cucumber	

Cut a lid off the rolls and take out the inside. Spread butter thickly inside the rolls. Chop the ham, tomato and cucumber finely. Moisten with sandwich spread or mayonnaise, adding a little made mustard. Fill the rolls and put them in the oven for 10 minutes at 200°C (400°F)/Gas 6. Garnish with cress.   *Serves 4.*

Amager Bread
Amagermad

This is the only native 'closed sandwich', made with a slice of rye bread sandwiched to a slice of French bread with a thick layer of Danish butter in between. It is amazing how good the two types of bread taste put together in this way. This 'sandwich' is said to have originated as a workman's lunch on the island of Amager, which forms part of Copenhagen.

Salads for Smørrebrød
Salater til smørrebrød

Mayonnaise salads are distinctive to the Danish cold kitchen, used both on *smørrebrød* and with the Cold Table. Most of them are usually bought ready-made but outside Denmark a little more effort has to be made. They are, however, not difficult to make at home.

Basic Mayonnaise
Almindelig mayonnaise

1 large egg yolk
300ml ($\frac{1}{2}$ pint) oil
5ml (1 tsp) vinegar or lemon juice
2.5ml ($\frac{1}{2}$ tsp) salt
pinch white pepper

The egg yolk and oil must be at room temperature. Using a wooden spoon or rotary whisk, beat the egg yolk until thick. Beating all the time, add the oil in a thin stream alternating with a few drops of vinegar or lemon juice. Continue until all the oil has been absorbed and a thick creamy textured mayonnaise is the result, then add the seasoning.

If the mayonnaise curdles add a little warm water and beat thoroughly to stabilize the mixture. Or take another egg yolk, beat it until thick and then slowly add the curdled mixture to the egg yolk in a thin stream, beating all the time. Continue with the basic recipe.

For a richer mayonnaise fold in 30ml (2 tbsp) whipped cream. To extend the mayonnaise fold in half a beaten egg white.

Curry Salad
Karrysalat

120ml (8 tbsp) basic mayonnaise
5ml (1 tsp) curry powder
5ml (1 tsp) Worcestershire sauce
5ml (1 tsp) chopped anchovy
30ml (2 tbsp) chopped hard-boiled egg
30ml (2 tbsp) chopped boiled macaroni or chicken

Mix all the ingredients together and serve heaped on buttered rye bread. Garnish with slices of hard-boiled egg as *smørrebrød* or, for the Cold Table, serve as an accompaniment for cooked ham. This quantity will make 2 *smørrebrød*.

Quick Rémoulade
Nem remoulade

To 150ml ($\frac{1}{4}$ pint) basic mayonnaise fold in 10ml (2 tsp) whipped cream. Add 15ml (1 tbsp) French mustard. Finely chop or sieve a hard-boiled egg and add to the mixture together with a finely chopped gherkin, a little mild onion, chopped, or drained and chopped capers.

Italian Salad
Italiensk salat

Turn a mixture of cooked diced vegetables, such as carrots, peas, potatoes, and capers in the basic mayonnaise. This is similar to Russian salad in Britain.

Spring Salad
Forårssalat

Blend tiny raw cauliflower florets, cooked peas, diced carrots and raw sliced mushrooms with a little basic mayonnaise.

Decorations
Pynt

Radish Roses Choose medium-sized radishes with fresh green tops. Leave a small leaf on each. Cut the skin of the radish in sections down from the root end towards the stalk, making 3–6 cuts, but do not cut through the whole radish. Place cut radishes in cold water until they open like flowers, in about 1 hour.

Twists or Butterflies Tomato, cucumber, beetroot, lemon and orange are suitable. Cut the fruit or vegetable into round slices and cut each slice through the centre leaving a good piece at the top holding the halves together. Twist halves in opposite directions and place in position on the *smørrebrød*.

If the tomato is rather soft, put a piece of cucumber on either side, cut through all 3 pieces as described above, twist and place all 3 pieces in position on the topping at once.

Tomato Snippets These are made from the ends of tomatoes which would otherwise be thrown away after cutting the slices or twists.

Onion Rings Choose a medium-sized onion, or the rings will be too big for the *smørrebrød*. Peel and cut the onion crosswise. Separate the rings and use them in graduated sizes as a garnish. Onion rings can also enclose another garnish such as chopped hard-boiled egg or diced beetroot. Use on herrings or with salami.

Gherkin Fans Make several cuts in the flower end of the gherkin towards the stalk end. Press slices apart to form a fan.

Egg Strips
Æggestrimler

2 eggs	*pinch salt*
90ml (6 tbsp) water or	*pepper*
thin cream	

Beat the eggs with the water or cream and strain them through a sieve. Season to taste. Butter an oblong tin such as a loaf tin, taking care that the mixture is only about 2cm ($\frac{3}{4}$in) thick. Put the tin in a water bath and cook for about 30 minutes in a low oven until set. Cool, turn out and cut in strips. Use as a garnish with ham, smoked fish, and *smørrebrød*.

Meat Jelly Strips
Sky

5ml (1 tsp) meat extract	*15g ($\frac{1}{2}$oz) gelatine*
300ml ($\frac{1}{2}$ pint) hot water	*dissolved in 15ml*
300ml ($\frac{1}{2}$ pint) meat stock	*(1 tbsp) hot water*

Dissolve the meat extract in the hot water, add stock and gradually pour in dissolved gelatine, stirring all the time. Pour the mixture into an oblong dish so that it is about 2cm ($\frac{3}{4}$in) thick and leave to set.

When cold turn out, cut into strips and use as a garnish with liverpâté, salami or pork.

The Cold Table and Festive Menus

1 Salami and spiced pork sausages with onion rings and meat jelly
2 *Tarteletter* with spinach and ham
3 Smoked eel with scrambled egg
4 Shrimps in mayonnaise
5 Hard-boiled egg with mayonnaise, mock caviar and shrimps
6 Roast beef with rémoulade sauce, fried onions
7 Herrings in curry sauce
8 Marinated herrings with onion ring and dill
9 Marinated herrings with soured cream dressing
10 Roast gammon with tomatoes filled with Italian salad
11 Liverpâté with bacon and mushrooms
12 Tomato salad
13 *Frikadeller* with potato salad
14 Roast pork with red cabbage
15 Roast chicken with cucumber salad
16 Danish cheese board
17 Fruit salad in melon
18 Various breads and Danish butter

The idea of the Cold Table (*Det Kolde Bord*) is to have a help-yourself meal on the table with the guests comfortably seated around it. One or more warm dish is always served, the other food being cold. The food is put out in great variety, but in smaller amounts than for a set meal when each course is served in sufficient quantities to give everyone a good helping. The rhythm of the multi-course meal being set aside, guests are invited to help themselves. They can eat as little or as much as they wish.

Most people start with a sharp fish taste – and herrings make a wonderful appetizer – switching later to meat, vegetables and salads, and later still to cheese or sweets. Clean plates are in constant supply so that the taste of one food does not disturb the flavour of the next.

Different breads are also served. These are buttered well and eaten with the food on the plate, or sometimes the food is put on top of the bread as in the style of *smørrebrød* and eaten that way.

The 'little warm dishes' – luncheon dishes – are brought in at appropriate moments. Only small portions are served to each person. They are not regarded as a main course because guests are expected to eat the various other foods on the table. The 'warm dishes' will be offered without potatoes in a private home, although in restaurants these dishes are sometimes garnished with vegetables.

All kinds of low bowls, deep glasses, china and earthenware plates and stainless steel dishes are used as containers for the food which is set in the centre of the table. Places are set around the food for guests, with knives and forks, the first plate, and glasses. If there is not enough room, the comfort of the guests comes first; they will be seated but only some of the food will be put out and the host and hostess will unobtrusively fetch further supplies as the meal progresses. Alternatively, side tables may be used.

97

At one end of the scale the Cold Table can be very simple, perhaps just two kinds of fish, two kinds of meat, one 'little warm dish', some salads, bread and butter and cheese. At the other end comes the Grand Cold Table with variety and luxury of banqueting proportions. These are served primarily in restaurants rather than the home and British readers can sample them at the Danish Food Centre restaurants in Manchester and Glasgow. In between these two extremes comes the party menu given here.

This chapter also includes some menus for special occasions, in keeping with the Danish love of celebration.

Party Cold Table
Selskabsbord

For 12 Persons

Quantities should be lavish. Any left-overs can be used for open sandwiches, salads and *réchauffé* dishes later.

Fish

Sunday herrings
Marinated salt herrings
Shrimps in mayonnaise, garnished with asparagus and cress
Smoked eel with scrambled egg
Hard-boiled eggs, halved and garnished with mayonnaise and shrimp

Small Salads

Curry salad
Rémoulade sauce
Italian salad
Cucumber salad
Red cabbage
Potato salad with chives
Sliced tomatoes with onion

Cold Meats and Sausages

Salami and spiced pork sausage with onion and meat jelly
Liverpâté with crisply fried bacon, fried onions and mushrooms
Roast chicken, cut in portions and garnished
Marinated bacon, decorated with lettuce and chopped meat jelly and served with halved tomatoes filled with Italian salad

Hot dishes

Spiced *frikadeller*
Tarteletter cases with creamed spinach and ham filling

Sweets

Kirsten's fruit salad
Lemon soufflé
Danish cheese board

Bread and Butter

French loaves
Granary bread
Rye bread or pumpernickel
Butter cut in slices or cubes (serve on ice in hot weather)

Drinks

Snaps: Aalborg Akvavit or Jubilæums Akvavit.
Lager: Carlsberg or Tuborg.
Liqueur: Cherry Heering cherry liqueur.

Birthday Cold Table
Fødselsdagsbord

This is a simple style of cold table with one warm dish. It serves 8–12.

325-g (11½-oz) jar marinated skinless herrings with soured cream dressing
325-g (11½-oz) jar marinated skinless herrings with raw onion rings
225-g (8-oz) can shrimps served on cooked rice
8–12 eggs, hard-boiled, halved and piped with a little mayonnaise, garnished with mock caviar
2 125-g (4½-oz) cans mackerel in tomato, decorated with lemon and cucumber slices
225g (8oz) salami slices garnished with raw, finely chopped onion
Biksemad, made with 1kg (2lb) meat
Mixed green salad
225g (8oz) potato salad
100g (4oz) Italian salad
100g (4oz) mayonnaise
100g (4oz) cucumber salad

Danish Cheese Board:
225g (8oz) Danish Brie
225g (8oz) Mycella cheese
225g (8oz) Esrom cheese

A Light Luncheon
En let frokost

This meal starts with herrings and potatoes and is followed by a cheese tray with bread, biscuits and butter. It will serve 8–10

2–3 325g (11½oz) jars marinated skinless herrings
Potato salad
300g (10oz) Danish Blue Cheese
300g (10oz) Danish Camembert or Brie
400g (14oz) Esrom cheese
150g (5oz) Mild Havarti cheese
125g (4oz) Liqueur flavoured Cream Cheese Roll

Christmas
Jul

Celebrations start with the appearance of Christmas trees in the town hall square. Illuminated garlands of fir are hung across the main streets. The traditional foods begin to appear such as a yeast Christmas cake and Christmas biscuits. The children count the days, opening tiny windows on an Advent calendar. The Christmas candle burns on the table, timed to become lower and lower until finally, when it is burned out, Christmas Eve has arrived.

Danes travel from all over the world to be home in time for the Christmas Eve dinner. It is the highlight of Christmas. The meal is served shortly after the afternoon church service, so that even the youngest member of the family can stay up for it. Afterwards come carols and dancing round the Christmas tree, followed by the present-giving.

Christmas Eve Dinner

Rice porridge with powdered cinnamon and butter, roast goose, duck, or pork with crackling, prune and apple stuffing, gravy, poached apple halves with redcurrant jelly, sugar-browned and plain boiled potatoes, red cabbage, green vegetable, ris à l'amande (if the 'porridge' is not served first) with cherry sauce, or a cold soufflé, coffee with almond fingers.

Christmas Day Cold Table   Juledagsbord

The Christmas Day lunch is the year's biggest Cold Table with meats from the Christmas Eve Dinner plus ham, fish, salami, other sausages and salads. Black pudding (blood sausage) and pork brawn are two specialities in all the food shops at Christmas time.

FISH: Marinated herrings with raw onions, herrings in curry sauce, dill herrings with finely chopped egg, sardines with lemon.

MEAT AND SAUSAGES: Cold goose, duck, or pork (from Christmas Eve Dinner), chicken in horseradish sauce (served hot) with triangles of fried bread, Christmas ham with salad, home-made liverpâté garnished with bacon and mushrooms, salami sausage with raw onion rings, cold tongue

SALADS: Red cabbage, poached apples with cooked prunes (from day before), chicory salad or green salad, as available, Italian salad, hard-boiled egg and tomato salad, mayonnaise, pickled beetroot, cucumber salad

CHEESE BOARD: See page 80

SWEET: Fruit salad, layer cake, Christmas biscuits

New Year's Eve
Nytårsaften

New Year's Eve is always celebrated with fireworks. It is the one night of the year when Danes like to go out, thus rewarding the housewife for her Christmas toil. Those who prefer to stay home tend to have dinner late, but they allow their children to stay up to see the fireworks and share the toasts.

Whole boiled cod (page 25) was once the all-dominating dish to follow the heavy Christmas fare, but nowadays a Cold Table or smørrebrød may be served.

TRADITIONAL MENU: Boiled cod, cheese board, lemon soufflé, almond fingers, coffee.

MODERN MENU: Herring collation or smørrebrød, hamburgerryg with kale or spinach in sauce, sugar-browned potatoes, cheese board, lemon soufflé, almond fingers, coffee.

Carnival
Fastelavn

On the Monday before Lent, Danish children wake their parents early in the morning by beating their beds with a Carnival Wreath of birchwood twigs decorated with strips of coloured paper and sweets. They do not stop beating until they are given an orange, a bun or better still 1 kroner! During the day the children, dressed in old clothes and other disguises, sing in the streets collecting money for further buns.

In the afternoon, the children act out a ceremony called 'beating the cat off the barrel'. A barrel, decorated with crêpe paper and filled with fruit and sweets, is hung from a tree. On top is a black toy cat. A black cat is considered unlucky in Denmark and in this ceremony it symbolizes the evil of which the world wants to be rid during Lent. The children beat the barrel with sticks, and the child who knocks the cat off is called the 'Cat's King' and is given a crown. The contents of the barrel are shared by everyone and there is a tea party afterwards with more buns.

Carnival Tea Party

Carnival buns with butter (page 105), hot chocolate with whipped cream, layer cake (page 109).

Easter

Påske

There is a public holiday in Denmark at Easter time, usually Maundy Thursday, Good Friday and Easter Monday. Eggs are decorated, or boiled and served in a mustard sauce; veal, chicken and sometimes lamb dishes are served.

Easter Menu

Herring collation, Easter veal or Easter chicken, peas and carrots in sauce, new potatoes with herbs (parsley, dill or chives) or mashed potatoes, cheese board, Manor House apple cake, Danish pastries and small cakes, coffee.

Midsummer's Night

St Hansaften

Midsummer's Night is celebrated on the Eve of St John's Day, June 24th. Parties are held around giant bonfires on which an effigy of a witch is burnt, and everyone sings traditional songs. Oddly enough there is no traditional fare. In modern Denmark a barbecue has become very popular.

Midsummer's Barbecue

Bacon-wrapped sausages, barbecued pork chops, green salad, potato salad, Danish pastries and small cakes, coffee.

Constitution Day

Grundlovsdag

Constitution Day, June 5th, celebrates the Danish Constitution of 1849 which transferred power from the King to the people. It was, for its time, one of the most liberal constitutions in Europe and the day is still celebrated as a public half-holiday with both official and private celebrations. Rhubarb pudding served with whipped cream is called on that day 'Constitution Day Pudding', its red and white colours representing the colours of the national flag, the *Dannebrog*.

Constitution Day Menu (5 courses)

Clear soup with meat balls, fish gratin, veal in dill, cheese board, mocca dessert and/or rhubarb pudding, coffee.

St Martin's Eve

Mortensaften

St Martin's Eve is an ingenious excuse for a bright food spot as winter hardens. It is celebrated on November 10th, and is quite simply a food tradition without frills. It is a night when goose or roast duck with prune and apple stuffing is always served. According to legend, St Martin tried to hide from his pursuers among his geese but they protested loudly and this led to his capture and eventual execution.

St Martin's Eve Menu

Green kale soup, roast goose or duck, sugar-browned and white potatoes, red cabbage, cheese board, veiled country lass and/or caramel ring with ice cream, almond fingers, coffee.

Danish Baking

By tradition the Danish housewife is a connoisseur of home baking. Her family love cakes and biscuits and a visitor to a Danish home for coffee can expect to have a happy time tasting a selection of delicious cookies and little cakes. Next to eating these mouth-watering goodies the Danish housewife enjoys baking them, especially around Christmas time when many traditional recipes are used.

Outside Denmark the best-known baking recipe must surely be Danish Pastries – or *Wienerbrød* as the Danes call them, which means Vienna bread. Today these pastries are frequently bought from the local baker but they are very inexpensive and not at all difficult to make at home.

Throughout Danish baking there is a frequent use of almonds, chopped, ground or in almond paste. The *Kransekager* or marzipan cake features particularly at festive occasions such as weddings and birthdays. These beautiful towering cakes are formed from graduated rings of marzipan placed on top of each other, starting with the largest ring and ending with the smallest. Finally the cake is iced with thin strips of white icing in a zigzag pattern. Sets of graduated baking tins are used to make the rings but the same mixture is often baked in fingers to serve with coffee after a meal.

Danish baking falls into three main categories: Danish pastries and other yeast recipes; loaf cakes and layer cakes; and small cakes and Christmas cookies. The main ingredient for all of them is the Danish butter. In Denmark the traditional Lurpak butter is used but elsewhere either this or the sweet-cream Danish butter called Danelea can be used.

When baking with butter there are a few useful tips to remember if you want to achieve especially fine results. For cakes made by the creaming method, bring the butter out of the refrigerator and let it soften to room temperature before using it. Then it creams quickly, which will give a better result. When a recipe calls for softened butter it should be worked with a palette-knife or beaten with a wooden spoon to a spreading consistency before beginning preparation.

Unsalted butter is usually best for butter creams although some people rather like the salty/sweet flavour that results from using a salted butter. It is a matter of personal taste.

Danish Pastries
Wienerbrød

15g (½oz) fresh yeast or 10ml (2 tsp) dried yeast and 2.5ml (½ tsp) sugar
90ml (6 tbsp) warm water
1 egg, beaten
225g (8oz) plain flour
2.5ml (½ tsp) sugar
pinch salt
25g (1oz) lard
150g (5oz) slightly salted butter

Blend the fresh yeast into the warm water. If using dried yeast, dissolve the sugar in the warm water, and then sprinkle on the yeast. Leave until frothy, about 15–20 minutes.

Add the beaten egg to the yeast liquid. Mix the flour, sugar and salt in a large mixing bowl. Rub the lard into the flour, add the yeast liquid and mix to a soft dough. Turn on to a floured board and knead until smooth. Place dough in a lightly oiled polythene bag and rest it in a cool place for about 10 minutes.

Soften the butter into a rectangle about 1cm (½in) thick. Roll out the dough to approximately 26cm (10in) square. Spread the butter down the centre of the square, fold the sides over the butter in the middle to overlap about 1cm (½in) and seal the bottom and top.

Karoline's Apple Cake (page 108)

103

Roll out the dough to an oblong strip approximately 45 × 15cm (18 × 6in). Fold evenly in three. Place the dough in the polythene bag and allow to rest for 10 minutes.

Turn out, ready to roll in the opposite direction. Repeat the rolling, folding and resting twice more. The dough is now ready for use.

To shape Danish pastries
The basic dough is sufficient for *any two* of the following variations.

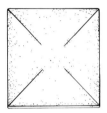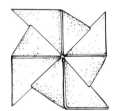

Windmills
40g (1½oz) almond paste, little beaten egg, raspberry jam

Roll out half the basic dough to a 20 × 30-cm (8 × 12-in) rectangle. Trim the edges and divide the dough into 6 10-cm (4-in) squares, using a ruler. Place the squares on a greased baking tray. Put a little almond paste in the centre of each square, and brush the paste lightly with a little of the beaten egg. Cut from the corner of each square to within 1cm (½in) of the centre. Fold alternate corners of each triangle thus formed towards the centre and press the points into the almond paste. Brush over with beaten egg, prove and bake. When cool, place raspberry jam in the centre of each pastry. *Makes 6.*

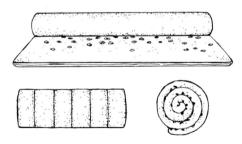

Fruit Snails
little beaten egg, 25g (1oz) butter, 25g (1oz) caster sugar, 5ml (1 tsp) cinnamon, 25g (1oz) sultanas, 50g (2oz) icing sugar, 5ml (1 tsp) water

Roll out half the basic dough to a 35 × 15-cm (15 × 6-in) rectangle. Brush the short edges with beaten egg.

Cream the butter with the caster sugar and cinnamon, spread this spiced butter on the dough and sprinkle with sultanas. Roll up from the short end to make a fat roll. Cut into 6 slices, and place on a greased baking sheet. Flatten slightly and brush with egg. Prove and bake. Decorate with water icing when cool.

To make the icing, sieve the icing sugar, blend in the water and beat until smooth. Trickle over the cooked pastries. *Makes 6.*

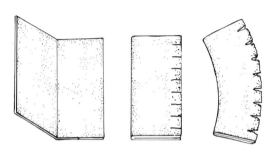

Cock's Comb
25g (1oz) butter, 25g (1oz) caster sugar, 25g (1oz) crushed macaroons (or 45ml (3 tbsp) apple purée or lemon curd), little beaten egg, 15g (½oz) chopped almonds

Roll out half the basic dough into a rectangle 20 × 30cm (8 × 12in). Cut into 6 10-cm (4-in) squares. Cream the butter with the caster sugar and add the macaroons. Place a little of the chosen filling in the centre of each square. Brush the edges with beaten egg, fold the dough in half and make 6–8 incisions along the edge. Bend each 'comb' so that the 'teeth' fan out. Brush with more egg and scatter with chopped almonds. Prove and bake. *Makes 6.*

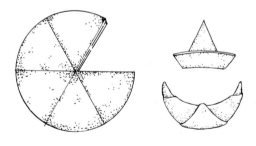

Pastry Horns
little beaten egg, 40g (1½oz) almond paste, 15g (½oz) chopped almonds

Roll out half the basic dough thinly into a circle 30cm (12in) in diameter. Trim the edge if necessary, and divide into 6 triangular sections. Brush the long sides of each piece with beaten egg. Place a little of the almond paste in the middle of the short side. Roll up towards the point and curve into a crescent shape. Place on a greased baking sheet and brush with beaten egg. Scatter with chopped almonds. Prove and bake. *Makes 6.*

To Prove Cover the pastries with greased polythene and allow them to rise in slight warmth for about 15–20 minutes until they are puffy and have doubled in size. Do not put them in the oven or too warm a place to prove, or the butter will run.

To Bake Remove the polythene and bake at 220°C (425°F)/Gas 7 for 12–15 minutes. Allow to cool before decorating. (Illustration pages 2 and 3.)

Butter Horns
Smørhorn

25g (1oz) fresh yeast or 15ml (1 tbsp) dried yeast and 5ml (1 tsp) sugar	1 egg
	400g (14oz) plain flour
	2.5ml (½ tsp) salt
	5ml (1 tsp) sugar
150ml (5fl oz) warm milk	little beaten egg
100g (4oz) melted and cooled butter	

Blend the fresh yeast into the warm milk. If using dried yeast, dissolve the sugar in the warm milk and sprinkle on the yeast. Leave until frothy, about 15–20 minutes.

Beat together the melted butter, egg and yeast liquid. Mix the flour, salt and sugar in a large mixing bowl. Add the liquid and mix to a firm dough. Knead well for about 5 minutes until dough is smooth and elastic.

Divide the dough in two. Roll each piece into a circle 36cm (14in) in diameter. Cut each circle into 8 triangles. Roll up each triangle, starting from the widest end. Curve round into a crescent and place on a greased baking tray. Brush with beaten egg.

Place the tray in a lightly oiled polythene bag and leave the dough to rise until it has doubled in size: 1–1½ hours in a warm place, 2 hours at room temperature.

Remove the polythene and bake in a very hot oven, 230°C(450°F)/Gas 8, for approximately 12 minutes.

To serve, cut in half and spread with butter. *Makes 16.*

Poppy Seed Rolls
Tebirkes

25g (1oz) fresh yeast or 15ml (1 tbsp) dried yeast and 5ml (1 tsp) sugar	450g (1lb) plain flour
	2.5ml (½ tsp) salt
	15ml (1 tbsp) granulated sugar
225ml (8fl oz) warm milk	30ml (2 tbsp) poppy seeds
250g (9oz) butter	

Blend the fresh yeast into the warm milk. If using dried yeast, dissolve the sugar in the milk and sprinkle on the yeast. Leave until frothy, about 15–20 minutes.

Rub 150g (5oz) butter into the flour. Mix in the salt and sugar, add the yeast liquid and mix to a soft dough. Turn on to a lightly floured surface and knead until smooth and elastic, about 5 minutes. Place in a lightly oiled polythene bag and leave to rise for 20 minutes until slightly puffy.

On a lightly floured board roll the dough out into an oblong 20 × 50cm (19 × 20in). Soften the remaining butter and spread it along the length of the dough and halfway across the width. Fold over the other half of the dough to overlap slightly. Fold the top edge underneath the bottom edge to seal in the butter.

Brush with lightly beaten egg white and sprinkle with poppy seeds. Cut into 14 triangles. Place on greased baking trays. Bake in a very hot oven 230°C (450°F)/Gas 8 for 15 minutes.

Cut the rolls lengthwise and serve spread with butter for tea or breakfast. *Makes 14.*

Carnival Buns
Fastelavnsboller

15g (½oz) fresh yeast or 10ml (2 tsp) dried yeast and 5ml (1 tsp) sugar	40g (1½oz) raisins
	25g (1oz) mixed peel
	5ml (1 tsp) mixed spice or 2.5ml (½ tsp) ground cardamom
75ml (5 tbsp) warm milk	
275g (10oz) plain flour	
pinch salt	1 standard egg
75g (3oz) butter	little butter and crushed sugar cubes to finish
40g (1½oz) caster sugar	

Blend the fresh yeast into the warm milk. If using dried yeast, dissolve the sugar in the milk, and sprinkle on the yeast. Leave until frothy, about 15–20 minutes.

Place the flour and salt in a large bowl. Rub in the butter until the mixture resembles fine breadcrumbs. Add the sugar, raisins, peel and spice, and stir well.

Beat the egg and add it to the yeast liquid. Pour into the dry ingredients and mix to a soft dough. Turn on to a lightly floured surface and knead until smooth and elastic, about 10 minutes. Place in a lightly oiled polythene bag and allow to rest for 5 minutes.

Cut the dough into 40-g (1½-oz) pieces, shape into rounds and place on a greased baking tray. Allow plenty of space between each round. Place the tray in a lightly oiled polythene bag and leave in a warm place until the buns have doubled in size, about 40 minutes. Take buns from bag and bake at 220°C(425°F)/Gas 7 for 12–15 minutes until golden brown.

Remove buns from tray and leave to cool. Very lightly butter the tops of the buns and roll them in crushed sugar cubes to decorate. *Makes approximately 10 buns.* (Illustration page 107.)

Rye Bread
Rugbrød

In Denmark rye bread is usually made by a rather complicated method using a soured dough. The recipe here is more straightforward and should produce a firm loaf suitable for use with *smørrebrød*. Rye flour varies in quality and sometimes gives a sticky dough. In this event, add extra flour during the kneading. If the finished bread is too dry, add extra liquid when making up the recipe next time.

50g (2oz) fresh yeast or 25g (1oz) dried yeast and 5ml (1 tsp) sugar	30ml (2 tbsp) black treacle
250ml (½ pint) lukewarm water	900g (2lb) rye flour
250ml (½ pint) lukewarm milk	200g (7oz) strong plain flour
	15ml (1 tbsp) salt

Blend the fresh yeast into the lukewarm water. If using dried yeast, dissolve the sugar into the water and sprinkle on the yeast. Leave until frothy, about 10 minutes. Stir the milk and black treacle into the yeast liquid.

Mix the flours and salt together in a large mixing bowl. Add the yeast liquid and mix to a firm dough with a wooden fork. Remove from the bowl and knead for about 5 minutes until the dough is smooth.

Grease 2 large loaf tins. Divide the dough in two, shape into a roll and place in the greased loaf tins. Prick the shaped dough with a fork in several places to the bottom of the dough. Place in a lightly oiled polythene bag and leave to rise for about 2½ hours until well risen.

Bake at the top of a pre-heated oven 230°C(450°F)/Gas 8 for 15 minutes. Reduce heat to 200°C(400°F)/Gas 6 for 45–50 minutes until firm and brown. For a crustier loaf, remove the bread carefully from the tins and bake on a baking tray for the last 10–15 minutes.

Cool completely on a cooling tray, preferably overnight. Wrap in a ploythene bag and keep for one day before slicing. *Makes 2 large loaves.*

Danish Christmas Cake
Dansk julekage

25g (1oz) fresh yeast or 15ml (1 tbsp) dried yeast and 5ml (1 tsp) sugar	2.5ml (½ tsp) salt
	5ml (1 tsp) cinnamon
	15ml (1 tbsp) sugar
150ml (¼ pint) warm milk	225g (8oz) mixed dried fruit
100g (4 oz) butter	25g (1oz) flaked almonds
2 eggs, beaten	25g (1oz) crushed loaf sugar
450g (1lb) plain flour	

Blend the fresh yeast into half the warm milk. If using dried yeast, dissolve the sugar in half the warm milk and sprinkle on the yeast. Leave until frothy, about 15–20 minutes.

Add 75g (3oz) of the butter to the remaining milk and heat gently to melt. Combine yeast and milk mixtures with the beaten eggs. Mix flour, salt, cinnamon and sugar together. Add the mixed fruit. Stir in the liquid to form a soft dough. Turn on to a lightly floured surface and knead until smooth and elastic, about 10 minutes.

Roll out the dough to fit into a 28 × 18-cm (11 × 7-in) tin. Leave in a warm place to rise for 30–40 minutes, until double in size. Melt the remaining butter and brush over the top. Sprinkle the flaked almonds and crushed loaf sugar over the dough. Bake in the middle of the oven at 200°C(400°F)/Gas 6 for about 30 minutes.

This cake may be eaten plain the same day and buttered thereafter. (Illustration page 107.)

Honey Bread (page 108) and Lace Biscuits (page 112)

Vanilla Butter Biscuits (page 113), Sandcake (page 108) and Carnival Buns (page 105)

Christmas Cake (page 106), Vanilla Rings and Jewish Cakes (page 112)

Sandcake
Sandkage

Traditional recipes sometimes used as many as 12 eggs and required an hour's beating. Today's version is quicker and easier to make but still depends on plenty of butter and eggs for its flavour.

175g (6oz) butter	100g (4oz) cornflour
175g (6oz) caster sugar	2.5ml ($\frac{1}{2}$ tsp) vanilla
3 eggs	essence
125g (4oz)) plain flour	30ml (2 tbsp) milk to mix
5ml (1 tsp) baking powder	25g (1oz) flaked almonds

Preheat the oven to 180°C(350°F)/Gas 4. Line the length and ends of a large 1-kg (2-lb) loaf tin with lightly greased greaseproof paper.

Cream the butter and caster sugar until light and fluffy, then beat in the eggs one at a time. Gradually fold in the sieved flour, baking powder and cornflour. Add the vanilla and milk to give a soft dropping consistency.

Place the mixture in the tin and level the surface. Sprinkle on the flaked almonds. Bake the cake for $1\frac{1}{4}$ hours on the centre shelf of the oven until firm to the touch. Lift the cake out, remove the greaseproof paper and allow to cool. Sprinkle with icing sugar. (Illustration page 107.)

Honey Bread
Honningkage

This is a very old Danish recipe, popular with children.

125g (4oz) butter	5ml (1 tsp) cinnamon
175g (6oz) honey	5ml (1 tsp) ground cloves
175g (6oz) soft brown	5ml (1 tsp) ground ginger
sugar	50g (2oz) chopped
2 eggs	almonds
5ml (1 tsp) bicarbonate of	50g (2oz) chopped mixed
soda	peel
275g (10oz) plain flour	50g (2oz) seedless raisins

Preheat the oven to 150°C(300°F)/Gas 2. Line a large 1-kg (2-lb) loaf tin with greaseproof paper, brush with melted butter.

Place the butter, honey and sugar in a saucepan and heat gently to just melt. Remove from the heat.

Beat the eggs in a bowl. Dissolve the bicarbonate of soda in 15ml (1 tbsp) hot water, add to the eggs with the melted liquid, sift in the flour and spices, and add the remaining ingredients. Beat well and pour into prepared tin.

Cook for about $1\frac{1}{4}$ hours until a thin skewer inserted into the centre comes out clean. Remove from tin, allow to cool and serve sliced spread with butter. (Illustration page 107.)

Karoline's Apple Cake
Karolines æblekage

This is an apple cake with a sponge-cake base which should be baked and eaten the same day. Serve the cake lukewarm with morning coffee or afternoon tea.

150g (5oz) butter	125g (4oz) plain flour
150g (5oz) granulated	75g (3oz) semolina
sugar	4–5 firm eating apples
2 eggs	25g (1oz) melted butter

Preheat the oven to 220°C(425°F)/Gas 7. Grease a 25-cm (10-in) tin with removable base with butter.

Cream together the butter and sugar until light and fluffy. Add the lightly beaten eggs a little at a time until well mixed. Fold in the sieved flour and the semolina. Spread this firm mixture into the tin.

Peel the apples and cut them in half. Remove the cores. Make 4 cuts in each piece of apple halfway through from the round side. Press the cut halves into the cake. Brush with a little melted butter. Bake the cake for approximately 30 minutes until the apples are just cooked. Serve warm with whipped cream. (Illustration page 102.)

Almond Fingers
Kransekager

225g (8oz) ground	225g (8oz) icing sugar
almonds	whites of 2 large eggs

Preheat the oven to 180°C(350°F)/Gas 4. Well grease baking tray. Mix the almonds and sugar together and stir gently over a low heat for about 5 minutes. Allow to cool and mix in the unwhipped egg whites to form a stiff dough. Shape the mixture by hand into almond fingers approximately 7cm (3in) long. If the dough is soft enough, it can be piped directly on to the baking tray. Bake for 5–7 minutes, remove from oven and allow to cool. When cold, glaze with finely piped water icing in a zig-zag design. *Makes 25–30.*

Cinnamon Layer Cake
Kanellagkage

The layers of this cake are very thin and crisp, almost brittle. They are sandwiched together with whipped cream and decorated with chocolate icing.

300ml ($\frac{1}{2}$ pint) whipping | *1 small egg*
cream | *125g (4$\frac{1}{2}$oz) flour*
125g (4$\frac{1}{2}$oz) butter | *7.5ml (1$\frac{1}{4}$ tsp) cinnamon*
100g (3$\frac{1}{2}$oz) caster sugar

ICING:
100g (4oz) plain chocolate | *15ml (1 tbsp) hot water*
10ml (2 tsp) butter | *8–12 whole almonds*

Preheat the oven to 220°C(425°F)/Gas 7. Grease and line 3 20-cm (8-in) sandwich tins. Whip the cream stiffly and put to chill in the refrigerator.

Cream the butter and sugar until light in colour. Beat in the egg. Sieve flour and cinnamon together and fold into the creamed mixture. Pour the mixture equally into the prepared tins and bake for 8–10 minutes, on the centre shelf. Remove from the tins while still hot and allow to cool before decorating.

To make the icing, melt the chocolate in a basin over hot water, beat in the butter and hot water.

Assemble the cake in layers with the ice-cold whipped cream. Pour the icing over the top layer and decorate with split almonds around the edge.

Macaroons
Makroner

Macaroons are served with afternoon coffee or used in the famous Sarah Bernhardt cakes. They can also be crushed and added to the traditional apple cake.

1 large egg white | *15ml (1 tbsp) cornflour*
100g (4oz) caster sugar | *5ml (1 tsp) almond*
50–75g (2–3oz) ground | *essence (optional)*
almonds

Preheat the oven to 180°C(350°F)/Gas 4. Line a baking tray with oiled greaseproof paper.

Put the egg white in a mixing bowl and whisk until light and foamy. Add the caster sugar, 50g (2oz) ground almonds, the cornflour and the almond essence. Beat well together. Gradually add the remaining ground almonds, if necessary, to give a stiff mixture. (The amount needed depends on the size of the egg white.)

Place in a piping bag fitted with a 1-cm ($\frac{1}{2}$-in) plain nozzle. Pipe – or spoon – small mounds of the mixture on to the lined baking tray, leaving plenty of space between each one to allow for spreading. Bake until golden brown, about 10 minutes.

Remove on to a wire rack with a palette-knife and leave to cool. *Makes 10–12 medium-sized macaroons.*

Sarah Bernhardt Cakes
Sarah Bernhardt-kager

175g (6oz) cooking | *5ml (1 tsp) grated lemon*
chocolate | *peel*
75g (2$\frac{1}{2}$oz) butter, slightly | *2.5ml ($\frac{1}{2}$ tsp) caster sugar*
salted or unsalted | *or vanilla sugar*
1 large egg | *10–12 medium-sized*
| *macaroons (see above)*

Grate chocolate, and melt half in a basin over hot water. Melt the butter in a separate pan. Whip the egg with the grated lemon rind and sugar. Mix the cooled chocolate and butter together, and add the egg mixture. When this has thickened spread it over the base of the macaroons, and allow it to set. Melt the remaining chocolate, and pour this over the firm chocolate layer. Decorate each cake with an almond, blanched, or a walnut on the chocolate.

Tosca Cake
Toscakage

The Danish love of almonds is well satisfied by this crunchy almond topping on a light sponge base.

SPONGE:

125g (4oz) butter
125g (4oz) caster sugar
rind of 1 lemon, finely
  grated

2 eggs
75g (3oz) plain flour
2.5ml ($\frac{1}{2}$ tsp) baking
  powder

TOPPING:

75g (3oz) butter
75g (3oz) granulated
  sugar
50g (2oz) chopped
  almonds

15ml (1 tbsp) plain flour
10ml (2 tsp) single cream

Preheat the oven to 160°C(325°F)/Gas 3. Grease a 20–25-cm (8–10-in) spring form or loose-bottomed flan tin.

Cream together the butter and caster sugar and lemon rind until light and fluffy. Add the lightly beaten eggs a little at a time, beating well after each addition. Fold in the sieved flour and baking powder. Put the mixture into the prepared tin and bake on the centre shelf for 20 minutes, until the mixture is set.

Prepare the almond topping by melting the butter and stirring in the other ingredients. Allow the mixture to come to the boil before pouring it over the cake. Return the cake to the oven and bake for a further 15–20 minutes until golden brown. Serve slightly warm, with single cream.

Strawberry Cones
Kræmmerhuse

These crisp buttery cones make an eye-catching sweet for special occasions. Fill them with whipped cream and fresh strawberries just before serving.

125g (4$\frac{1}{2}$oz) butter,
  softened
125g (4$\frac{1}{2}$oz) caster sugar
2 eggs, separated
125g (4$\frac{1}{2}$oz) plain flour,
  sifted

fresh strawberries (use
  whole or half berries)
300ml ($\frac{1}{2}$ pint) whipped
  cream to fill cones
little sugar

Strawberry Cones

110

Pre-heat the oven to 200°C/400°F/Gas 6. Cream the butter and sugar together until light and fluffy. Beat in the egg yolks, one at a time. Stiffly whisk the egg whites. Fold in the flour and egg whites alternately.

Grease two baking trays and drop 3 teaspoonfuls of the mixture onto each tray allowing room to spread. Using the back of the spoon spread into thin rounds about 7.5cm (3in) in diameter. Bake one tray at a time for 5–6 minutes until the outer edges just begin to brown.

Using a palette knife quickly remove the rounds from the tray. Curl each round a cream horn tin. Place on a cooling rack and allow to cool. The cones set quickly so that the horn tins can be re-used. Continue cooking remainder of mixture, washing and regreasing the trays between batches.

To serve, fill each cone with a spoonful of whipped cream, and decorate with a whole or half strawberry. To keep cones upright use sugar in the bottom of the serving dish to balance them. (It can be sifted and re-used afterwards.) *Makes about 24.*

Danish Cheese Cake
Dansk ostekage

This is not an American-style cheese cake but a cake iced with sweetened cream cheese. The base is a light fruit mixture with finely grated carrot added – an old trick for providing added texture and moisture in a cake. It's quick to make, too, as there is no creaming to do. Instead the butter is gently melted and the other ingredients added.

150g (5oz) butter
200g (7oz) caster sugar
175g (6oz) carrots, peeled
   and finely grated
2.5–5ml ($\frac{1}{2}$–1 tsp) salt
5ml (1 tsp) ground
   cinnamon

2 large eggs
200g (7oz) plain flour
15ml (1 tbsp) baking
   powder
100g (4oz) seedless raisins

ICING:
50g (2oz) butter, softened
100g ($3\frac{1}{2}$oz) cream
   cheese

100g (4oz) icing sugar,
   sieved
2.5ml ($\frac{1}{2}$ tsp) vanilla
   essence

Gently melt the butter and pour into a mixing bowl. Beat in the sugar, grated carrot, salt, ground cinnamon and eggs. Sieve the flour and baking powder and fold

Hazlenut Butter Biscuits (front), Orange Biscuits (left) and Jewish Cakes (pages 112–13)

Danish Cheese Cake

111

into the carrot mixture with the raisins. Pour into a well-buttered 16 × 20-cm (6½ × 8-in) tin.

Bake at 160°C(325°F)/Gas 3, on the centre shelf, for 40–45 minutes. Test by pressing lightly with the fingertips. The cake should be firm. Allow to cool for 5 minutes before turning out on to a cooling rack to become quite cold.

Beat the softened butter and cream cheese together until smooth, then gradually beat in the sieved icing sugar and vanilla essence. Leaving the cake bottom side up, spread the icing evenly over the sides and top. Make a decorative pattern with a fork.
(Illustration page 111.)

Hazelnut Butter Biscuits
Hasselnødssmåkager

150g (5oz) butter	2.5ml (½ tsp) baking
75g (3oz) granulated	powder
sugar	75g (3oz) hazelnuts, finely
175g (6oz) plain flour	chopped

Cream the butter and sugar until soft. Sieve the flour and baking powder, and fold into the creamed butter. Add chopped nuts and knead lightly. Cover and place the dough in the refrigerator for 30 minutes.

Preheat the oven to 200°C(400°F)/Gas 6. Shape the mixture into small balls and place them well apart on a greased baking tray. Press the top of the biscuits with a fork in two directions to make a grille pattern. Bake the biscuits for 7–8 minutes. *Makes about 60.*
(Illustration page 111.)

Butter Biscuits
Småkager

There's no substitute for good, rich butter to give these tempting biscuits crispness and flavour. Serve them whenever friends drop in for coffee or tea, or make them for Christmas as they do in Denmark. The biscuits will keep well if stored in an air-tight tin.

225g (8oz) plain flour	125g (4oz) granulated
2.5ml (½ tsp) baking	sugar
powder	2.5ml (½ tsp) vanilla
175g (6oz) butter	essence
	1 large egg, beaten

Sift flour and baking powder. Rub in the butter evenly. Stir in the sugar and vanilla. Mix in two tablespoons of the beaten egg to make a soft, smooth dough. Knead on a lightly floured surface, divide dough into three equal portions, and use to make Jewish Cakes, Vanilla Rings, and Finnish Bread.

Jewish Cakes

Roll out 1 portion of the butter biscuit dough very thinly on a floured working surface. Cut into rounds with a 5-cm (2-in) cutter. Place well apart on a greased baking tray and brush with beaten egg. Sprinkle with a mixture of 2.5ml (½ tsp) cinnamon, 15ml (1 tbsp) sugar and 15ml (1 tbsp) chopped almonds. Bake at 190°C (375°F)/Gas 5, on the centre shelf, for 8–9 minutes until firm. Bake in two batches if necessary. *Makes about 22.* (Illustration page 107.)

Vanilla Rings

Into another portion of the butter biscuit dough knead 25g (1oz) butter, 25g (1oz) ground almonds and 2.5ml (½ tsp) vanilla essence. Place in a forcing bag with a small star tube and pipe rings about 5cm (2in) in diameter well apart on to a greased baking tray. Bake at 190°C (375°F)/Gas 5 on the centre shelf for 9 minutes until firm and honey coloured. *Makes about 22.* (Illustration page 107.)

Finnish Bread

Roll out remaining portion of the butter biscuit dough into a long roll about 2.5cm (1in) wide. Square off by pressing the rounded sides to flatten slightly. Chill for 10 minutes. Cut slantwise into 1-cm (½-in) slices. Place on a greased baking tray placed well apart, brush with a little beaten egg and sprinkle with granulated sugar. Bake at 190°C(375°F)/Gas 5 on the centre shelf for 10 minutes until firm and a pale honey colour. *Makes 10–12.*

Lace Biscuits
Kniplingskager

100g (4oz) butter	pinch salt
100g (4oz) granulated	few drops vanilla essence
sugar	or 1.25ml (¼ tsp)
100g (4oz) rolled oats	ground ginger

Cream the butter and sugar till light and soft. Stir in the oats and flavouring and blend to a fairly stiff mixture. Roll the dough into small balls and place them on a greased baking tray, leaving a good space between each. Flatten each ball slightly with a palette-knife. Bake on the centre shelf of the oven at 200°C(400°F)/Gas 6 for 5–6 minutes, till golden brown round the edges. Leave to cool slightly on baking tray, then transfer carefully to a wire rack. *Makes 25–30.* (Illustration page 107.)

Klejner
Klejner

Small crisp biscuits, another Christmas favourite, which are deep fried rather than oven baked. They should be eaten the day they are made

65g (2½oz) slightly salted   1 large egg
   butter   15ml (1 tbsp) cream
250g (9oz) plain flour   vegetable oil or fat for
75g (3oz) caster sugar   frying
grated rind of ½ lemon

Rub butter into the flour until lightly mixed. Add the sugar and lemon rind. Work in the beaten egg and cream to form a dough and knead until well mixed. Cover and place in the refrigerator for 2–3 hours until well chilled.

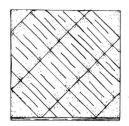

Roll out the dough very thinly and cut into diagonal strips 8 × 2.5cm (3½ × 1in). Make a 2-cm (¾-in) cut in the centre of each strip through which one end of the dough is pulled. Leave in a cool place to rest. Fry in hot fat until golden brown, turning once or twice. Drain on kitchen paper. If liked, toss in caster sugar and cinnamon. Serve when cool and crisp. *Makes 42.*

Orange Biscuits
Orangesmåkager

200g (7oz) butter   rind of 2 oranges, grated
250g (9oz) plain flour   100g (4oz) dark
50g (2oz) granulated   chocolate
   sugar

Rub the butter into the flour. Add sugar and finely grated orange rind. Form into a dough and knead lightly. Place the dough in the refrigerator for 1 hour. Preheat the oven to 200°C(400°F)/Gas 6.

Roll out the dough thinly to a rectangle. Cut it into oblong biscuits about 5 × 2.5cm (2 × 1in). Remove the biscuits one by one and place them on a greased baking tray.

Bake for 10 minutes, or until light brown. When baked dip one end of the biscuits in melted chocolate. *Makes about 40.* (Illustration page 111.)

Vanilla Butter Biscuits
Vaniljesmåkager

225g (8oz) butter   pinch salt
175g (6oz) caster sugar   10ml (2 tsp) vanilla
350g (12oz) plain flour   essence
5ml (1 tsp) baking powder

Work the butter with a wooden spoon to soften it a little and knead in the remaining ingredients. Knead well together and form into 2 neat rolls about 5cm (2in) in diameter. Roll up carefully in 2 pieces of foil and chill for about 1 hour or until required.

To bake the biscuits, preheat the oven to 190°C (375°F)/Gas 5. Cut the dough into as many 0.5-cm (¼-in) thick slices as you need. Store the remaining dough in the refrigerator for later use. Lightly butter a baking tray and arrange the slices well apart. Cook near the top of the oven for 15 minutes until lightly browned. Allow to cool and crisp on the baking tray before placing them on a cooling rack.

When cold sprinkle with icing sugar. These biscuits keep well in an airtight tin. The dough will keep at least two weeks in a refrigerator and even longer in a freezer. *Makes about 40.* (Illustration page 107.)

Puddings and Desserts

Every Dane seems to be born with a sweet tooth but sugar is expensive and these recipes, although often rich with cream, are seldom excessively sugared. Nor is a rich pudding eaten every day. They are reserved for special occasions, perhaps a birthday or dinner party. On ordinary days fruit yoghurts are popular and stewed fruit in summer or pancakes in winter are often served.

Ice cream is served all the year round. Danish ice cream is made from real cream and is extremely tasty and nutritious. The Danes sometimes accompany it with macaroons. Nougat-flavoured ice cream is a favourite.

The best known of Danish desserts, perhaps because Danes enjoy asking foreigners to pronounce its tongue-twisting name, is *rødgrød med fløde* – red fruit jelly with cream. This is absolutely delicious and need not necessarily be served with cream; it is just as nice with milk.

Almonds feature strongly in Danish puddings and desserts. It is traditional at Christmas time to eat a rice pudding into which a whole almond has been placed. This is not a rice pudding as we know it, because chopped almonds and whipped cream are mixed into the rice. The almonds give a nutty flavour and they also help to disguise the whole almond in the bowl. The person who gets the whole almond wins the *mandelgave* (almond prize). Most people, children especially, are so keen to win the prize that they will eat bowl after bowl of the rice pudding until the dish is clean and they have found the almond. This particular rice pudding is also served with a hot fruit sauce.

There is another rice pudding, or rice porridge, which in the olden days was eaten before the main course. The reason for this was that it took the edge off one's appetite so less of the more expensive meat course was required. This rice porridge is also the one put out for the *Julenisser* (Christmas fairies) who deliver the presents, a custom which is particularly strong in the country at Christmas time.

Danes seem to love apple, and there must be hundreds of variations to the traditional apple cake recipe. In fact, this is not a cake at all, but layers of puréed apple and toasted breadcrumbs or crumbled rye bread topped with whipped cream and perhaps chocolate flakes or slivers of redcurrant jelly. It is usually eaten lukewarm.

Lemon Soufflé
Citronfromage

15g (½oz) powdered gelatine	75g (3oz) sugar
juice and rind of 1 lemon	100ml (scant ¼ pint) whipping cream for
4 eggs	decoration

Soak the gelatine in the lemon juice in a bowl. Separate the eggs, and whisk the whites stiffly. Place the gelatine mixture over a pan of hot water and heat gently until it dissolves. Remove from the heat. Stir in the egg yolks and grated rind. Fold the sugar into the whites. When the gelatine mixture begins to thicken fold in the egg whites.

Pour into a glass dish, and when set decorate with the whipped cream. *Serves 4–5.*

Macaroon Ice Cream (page 121)

Tiger Soufflé

Tiger Soufflé

This dish gets its name from the striped effect of the ingredients when assembled. The Danes are very fond of sherry or rum-flavoured soufflés.

3 egg yolks	*10ml (2 tsp) cocoa*
60ml (4 tbsp) sugar	*4 egg whites*
15g ($\frac{1}{2}$oz) powdered	*whipped cream*
* gelatine*	*strawberries*
15ml (1 tbsp) rum	

Whisk the egg yolks until pale with the sugar and divide this mixture in half. Dissolve the gelatine in 45ml (3 tbsp) hot water together with the rum. Stir gently for a couple of minutes and divide in two equal parts. Mix one portion of the rum-flavoured gelatine with the cocoa and add to one half of the whisked yolks. Mix in two stiffly whisked egg whites. Then whisk the last two egg whites until stiff and combine them with the remaining portion of the yolk mixture and rum flavoured gelatine.

Put alternate layers of the brown and white mixtures in tall glasses and allow it to stiffen – say 3 hours. Decorate just before serving with whipped cream and strawberries. *Serves 4.*

Creamed Rice

Ris a l'amande

600ml (1 pint) milk	*about 15ml (1 tbsp) sugar*
60ml (4 tbsp) pudding rice	*about 150ml ($\frac{1}{4}$ pint) thick*
$\frac{1}{4}$ vanilla pod	* cream*
8–10 blanched almonds	*5ml (1 tsp) sherry*

Rinse a thick-bottomed saucepan with water and bring the milk to the boil in it. Wash the rice and place it in the boiling milk with the vanilla pod. Stir constantly for the first 5 minutes, then cover the saucepan with a lid and turn down the heat. Simmer the rice slowly for $\frac{3}{4}$ hour, stirring occasionally. When cooked, remove the vanilla and allow the rice to cool.

Chop the almonds and stir them into the rice together with the sugar. Whip the cream and when the rice is cold, stir in the whipped cream and sherry. Serve plain or with cherry sauce (page 121). *Serves 4.*

Rice Porridge

Risengrød

1.5 litres (2$\frac{1}{2}$ pints) milk	*5ml (1 tsp) cinnamon*
225g (8oz) pudding rice	*50g (2oz) butter*
5ml (1 tsp) salt	*1 large whole almond*
25g (1oz) sugar	* (optional)*

Bring the milk to the boil, add the rice and stir until the milk returns to the boil. Simmer for $\frac{3}{4}$–1 hour, until the rice is cooked and has absorbed the milk.

Add the salt. Mix together the sugar and cinnamon. Cut the butter in small pieces. Serve each portion with a knob of butter in the middle and sprinkle some of the cinnamon sugar over the top. At Christmas time remember to add the whole almond before serving (page 115). *Serves 6–8.*

Rice Fritters

Klatkager

225g (8oz) cold rice	*25g (1oz) chopped*
* porridge*	* almonds*
2 eggs	*25g (1oz) flour*
25g (1oz) raisins	*butter for frying*
grated rind of $\frac{1}{2}$ lemon	

Mix together all the ingredients except the butter. If the mixture is very stiff add a little milk. Using a dessertspoon drop the mixture in spoonfuls into a hot buttered frying pan, and fry on both sides. Sprinkle with sugar and serve with jam. *Makes 12.*

Caramel Ring

Karamelrand

225g (8oz) caster sugar
   flavoured with vanilla
200ml (7fl oz) water
500ml (18fl oz) milk

5 eggs
vanilla ice cream to fill
   the centre
double cream

Heat 200g (7oz) of the sugar in a heavy medium-sized saucepan. When it begins to brown, stir gently until it is all a light caramel colour. Take care not to let the heat build up at this stage or the caramel will burn. Pour this caramel into a 1-litre (1¾-pint) warmed ring mould and turn the mould quickly to cover it with caramel. Pour excess caramel back into the saucepan, add the water and simmer gently, stirring, to dissolve. Reduce a little to thicken, and allow this sauce to cool.

Heat the milk slightly and mix with the beaten eggs and remaining vanilla sugar. Strain the mixture and pour it into the prepared ring mould. Cover with foil. Fill a roasting tin one-third full with water, put in the mould and bake for 2 hours or until set at 125°C (250°F)/Gas ½. Cool the baked caramel custard and turn out when required on to a round serving dish. Fill the centre with the ice cream and pour some caramel sauce from the pan over it. Whip remaining sauce into the cream to serve separately. *Serves 6–8.*

Rhubarb Pudding

Rabarbergrød

Rhubarb is well-loved in Denmark, as its early arrival heralds the beginning of spring.

500g (1lb) rhubarb
100g (4oz) sugar
300–450ml (½–¾) pint
   water

½ vanilla pod
whipping cream or
   custard

Cut the rhubarb into 5-cm (2-in) pieces. Boil the sugar and water together, add the rhubarb and vanilla. Bring slowly to the boil, cover, take off heat and leave for 15 minutes.

Remove the rhubarb with a slotted spoon and place in a dish. Boil the juice to thicken a little. A little cornflour or arrowroot can be added to thicken the pudding if required. Mix 15ml (1 tbsp) in a little cold water, stir into rhubarb juice, bring to the boil and stir until thickened and clear. Pour over the pieces of rhubarb.

Decorate with whipped cream or custard. Cooked stoned prunes filled with a blanched almond are sometimes added on top of the pudding. *Serves 3–4.*

Kirsten's Fruit Salad

Kirstens frugtsalat

425-g (15-oz) can fruit
   cocktail
30ml (2 tbsp) mayonnaise

90ml (6 tbsp) whipped
   double cream

Carefully drain the canned fruit reserving a few pieces for garnish. Fold the mayonnaise into the whipped cream. Blend the fruit into this mixture so that it is completely covered.

Fresh fruit salad finely cut can be used. The proportion of the cream mixture should be one-third mayonnaise to two-thirds whipped cream.

Serve in a glass bowl which should be decorated with reserved fruit, or in a melon shell. This mixture can also be used as a Danwich topping on buttered bread with lettuce. *Serves 4.*

Veiled Country Lass

Bondepige med slør

750g (1½lb) apples
100g (4oz) butter
100g (4oz) sugar
175g (6oz) grated rye
   bread or crushed
   digestive biscuits

150–300ml (¼–½ pint)
   whipping cream
grated chocolate

Thinly slice the apples and stew them gently with 50g (2oz) butter and 50g (2oz) sugar, but no water. Mix the grated rye bread or digestive biscuits with the remaining sugar and fry lightly in the remaining butter. Place alternate layers of apple and rye bread in a bowl, finishing with a layer of rye bread mixture. Decorate with whipped cream and grated chocolate. *Serves 4–5.*

117

Orange and Lemon Cheese Cake
Appelsin- og citronostekage

200g (7oz) processed
    cream cheese
150ml (¼ pint) soured
    cream
100g (4oz) caster sugar
2.5ml (½ tsp) vanilla
    essence
1 packet lemon jelly

50g (2oz) unsalted butter
100g (4oz) plain biscuits
150ml (¼ pint) double
    cream
chocolate buttons
mandarin orange
    segments

Cream the cheese and add the soured cream, sugar and vanilla essence. Dissolve the jelly in 150ml (¼ pint) hot water and allow to cool slightly. Melt the butter. Crush the plain biscuits and blend well with the melted butter. Press biscuit mixture on to the bottom of a 20-cm (8-in) cake tin which has a removable base. Whip the double cream until fairly thick and combine it with the cream cheese mixture. Fold in the lemon jelly and pour the mixture into the cake tin. Allow to set in the refrigerator. Before serving, decorate the sides with chocolate buttons and the top with drained segments of mandarin orange. This cake can be made the day before serving. *Makes 6–8 portions.*

Danish Apple Cake
Dansk æblekage

Danish cookery books give many versions of this popular apple pudding. The buttered crumbs can be made in advance and kept in an air tight jar. Use them for this recipe or sprinkle them over stewed or canned fruit. Crushed digestive biscuits fried in butter make a quick and pleasant alternative to the white bread-crumbs.

750g (1½lb) cooking
    apples
75g (3oz) butter
100g (4oz) fresh
    breadcrumbs

75g (3oz) granulated
    sugar
150ml (¼ pint) whipping
    cream
redcurrant jelly

Peel and core the apples, slice them and cook slowly with just enough water to cover the bottom of the pan. When soft mash the apples to a purée with a fork, adding 25g (1oz) butter and sugar to taste if the apples are tart. Leave it cool.

Melt the remaining butter in a frying pan, add the breadcrumbs and sugar and fry until golden.

Just before serving arrange alternate layers of apples and crumbs in a glass bowl, finishing with a layer of crumbs. Decorate with whipped cream and redcurrant jelly. *Serves 4.*

Raspberry and Orange Meringue
Marengsbund med appelsincreme og hindbær

5ml (1 tsp) cornflour	grated rind of 1 orange
5ml (1 tsp) vanilla essence	5ml (1 tsp) orange juice
5ml (1 tsp) white vinegar	150ml ($\frac{1}{4}$ pint) double
3 egg whites	cream
200g (7oz) caster sugar	225–350g (8–12oz) fresh
50g (2oz) butter	raspberries
100g (4oz) icing sugar	

Blend the cornflour, vanilla essence, and vinegar in a cup. Whisk egg whites until stiff, whisk in a little sugar, then fold in the remainder with the blended cornflour. Cover a baking tray with oiled greaseproof paper and sprinkle it with caster sugar. Shape meringue mixture into a circle about 4cm (1$\frac{1}{2}$in) thick on the baking tray and cook it for one hour at 140°C (275°F)/Gas 1. Switch off oven and leave meringue to cool in the oven for 1 hour. Remove from oven, cool, and tear off paper.

Cream butter and icing sugar, add the grated orange rind and beat in the juice. Whisk the double cream until softly stiff and fold it into the butter cream. Spread this over the meringue and finally cover the top with the raspberries. *Serves 6.*

Cream Pudding with Strawberries
Føderand med jordbær

15g ($\frac{1}{2}$oz) powdered gelatine	50g (2oz) almonds
45ml (3 tbsp) cold water	300ml ($\frac{1}{2}$ pint) double cream
300ml ($\frac{1}{2}$ pint) milk	fresh or frozen
$\frac{1}{2}$ vanilla pod	strawberries or other
75g (3oz) sugar	fruit

Sprinkle gelatine in the cold water and soak for 5 minutes. Boil the milk with the split vanilla pod and the sugar. Remove pan from the heat, take out vanilla pod, add soaked gelatine, and stir to dissolve. Add peeled, chopped almonds. Leave to cool.

Whisk the double cream until it is rather stiff and turn it into the cooled milk. Pour the mixture into a circular 850-ml (1$\frac{1}{2}$-pint) mould and place it in the refrigerator for a few hours.

Just before serving, turn the cream pudding on to a dish. Decorate with fresh or frozen strawberries or other fruit. *Serves 4–6.*

Manor House Apple Cake
Herregårdsæblekage

175g (6oz) butter	2.5ml ($\frac{1}{2}$ tsp) salt
250g (9oz) flour	100g (4oz) sugar
	1 egg

FILLING:

1kg (2lb) cooking apples	75g (3oz) raisins
75g (3oz) sugar	25g (1oz) chopped almonds

TOPPING:

75g (3oz) butter	25g (1oz) chopped
75g (3oz) sugar	almonds

Rub the butter into the flour. Add the salt, sugar and egg and knead together. Leave to chill for about 1 hour before rolling to a thickness of 0.5cm ($\frac{1}{4}$in).

Cut two circles from the pastry to fit a 25-cm (10-in) spring form tin. Lightly grease the tin and lay one circle in the bottom. (The other is used as the 'lid'.) Re-roll the remaining pastry into strips 4cm (1$\frac{1}{2}$in) wide and use to line the sides of the tin.

Peel and core the apples and cut them into thin slices. Arrange them evenly in the pastry-lined tin, sprinkle with sugar, raisins and chopped almonds. Put the pastry 'lid' on top and press it well to the edge.

Cream the butter and sugar for the topping and add the chopped almonds. Spread this over the top and prick with a fork.

Bake in a preheated oven, 200°C(400°F)/Gas 6, for 45–50 minutes until golden brown. Serve lukewarm with whipped cream. *Serves 6–8.*

Blackcurrant Pancakes
Pandekager med solbærsyltetøj

150g (5oz) flour	25g (1oz) butter
5ml (1 tsp) sugar	50g (2oz) butter for
5ml (1 tsp) cardamom	frying
powder	blackcurrant jam
2 eggs	small block of ice
450ml ($\frac{3}{4}$ pint) milk	cream (optional)

Mix the flour, sugar and cardamom together in a bowl. Beat the eggs, add to the flour and gradually stir in the milk. Heat 25g (1oz) butter until it is just melted, and pour into the batter. This batter must not be too thick. Pour it into a jug.

Melt the butter for frying in a little pan. Warm the frying pan well, put in a spoonful of the melted butter, and pour in a little batter. Do not pour more batter than can, with a quick turn of the wrist, be made to cover the bottom of the pan in a thin layer. When the pancake begins to stiffen at the edge and turn brown, loosen it and turn it over, putting a little more butter in the pan. Fry until golden on both sides. Remove and keep hot. Continue until all the batter has been used. Serve immediately, filling each pancake with the jam and, if liked, some ice cream. *Makes 10.*

Orange Butter Pancakes
Pandekager med orangesmør

125g (4oz) plain flour	300ml ($\frac{1}{2}$ pint) milk
pinch salt	75g (3oz) butter
1 egg	

ORANGE BUTTER:

125g (4oz) butter	rind and juice of 1 orange
50g (2oz) sugar	miniature bottle Grand
grated rind of 1 lemon	Marnier

Use the flour, salt, egg and milk to prepare the batter, and stir in 40g (1$\frac{1}{2}$oz) melted butter. Beat smooth and leave until needed. Cream 125g (4oz) butter and sugar. Add lemon and orange rind, orange juice and Grand Marnier a little at a time.

Make small thin pancakes, using remaining butter to coat the frying pan and following the instructions for blackcurrant pancakes. Remove, fold into four and keep hot. Melt the orange butter in a large pan, put in the pancakes and heat them gently before serving. *Makes 8.*

Macaroon Ice Cream

Is med makroner

4–6 macaroons, about
    100g (4oz)
30ml (2 tbsp) sherry
25g (1oz) blanched
    almonds

knob butter
large block vanilla
    ice cream
150ml ($\frac{1}{4}$ pint) whipping
    cream

Slightly crush the macaroons and pour the sherry over them. Leave to soak for 2 hours. Cut the almonds lengthwise and fry in the butter until light brown. Cut the ice cream into pieces and pile it on to a dish in layers with the macaroons. Decorate with whipped cream and almonds. *Serves 4.*
(Illustration page 114.)

Fresh Cherry Sauce

Frisk kirsebærsauce

100g (4oz) sugar
300ml ($\frac{1}{2}$ pint) water
225g (8oz) cherries

25g (1oz) potato flour or
    arrowroot

Melt the sugar in the water and let it boil for 5 minutes to make a syrup. Wash and stone the cherries and cook them in the syrup until tender. Mix the potato flour to a smooth paste with a little water, add to the sauce and stir until lightly thickened. Do not boil. If using arrowroot, return pan to the heat, bring to the boil, and simmer for 2 minutes until clear. Serve with creamed rice, ice cream, or pancakes.

Quick Cherry Sauce

Nem kirsebærsauce

400-g (14-oz) can cherries
100ml (4fl oz) water

15ml (1 tbsp) cornflour

Bring the cherries, juice and 50ml (2fl oz) of the water to the boil. Stir the cornflour with the remaining water. Add this to the sauce and cook for 1 minute. Serve the sauce lukewarm.

Raspberry Trifle

Hindbærdessert

100g (4oz) macaroons or
    ratafia biscuits
225g (8oz) packet frozen
    raspberries, thawed

60ml (4 tbsp) sugar
300ml ($\frac{1}{2}$ pint) whipping
    cream
30ml (2 tbsp) sherry

Crush the macaroons and put them in a glass dish. Reserving a few whole raspberries for decoration, arrange the remainder over the macaroons, sprinkle with half the sugar and allow to soak for a while.

Whip the cream, not too stiffly, and carefully stir in the remaining sugar and the sherry. Pour this over the raspberries and leave to chill. Decorate with whole raspberries and serve. *Serves 6.*

Mocca Mousse

Mokkamousse

15g ($\frac{1}{2}$oz) powdered
    gelatine
100ml (4fl oz) water
3 eggs
75g (3oz) sugar
125g (4oz) cooking
    chocolate, grated

5ml (1 tsp) instant coffee
300ml ($\frac{1}{2}$ pint) whipping
    cream, or 150ml
    ($\frac{1}{4}$ pint) double cream
    and 150ml ($\frac{1}{4}$ pint)
    single cream
extra whipping cream

Soak the gelatine in the water in a bowl. Whisk the eggs and sugar until light and fluffy. Gently heat the gelatine over a pan of hot water until dissolved. Mix in the chocolate and the instant coffee. Stir the chocolate mixture into the eggs and sugar. Whip the cream stiffly and fold into the other ingredients. Pour into a glass dish and leave to set. Decorate with the extra whipped cream. *Serves 5–6.*

Red Fruit Jelly with Cream

Rødgrød med fløde

Rødgrød is usually made with several soft fruits as here, or sometimes with strawberries or rhubarb on their own.

750g (1½lb) mixed soft
    fruits – redcurrants,
    raspberries,
    blackcurrants,
    strawberries

15–30ml (1–2 tbsp) potato
    flour or arrowroot to
    each 600ml (1 pint) of
    juice
225g (8oz) sugar
25g (1oz) almonds

Clean the fruit and rinse it well in cold water. Place it in a large pan and add just enough cold water to cover. Simmer the fruit for 5 minutes until soft but not broken. Sieve the fruit, measure juice and weigh out potato flour or arrowroot. Dissolve sugar in juice over a gentle heat.

Blend the potato flour or arrowroot with a little water, and stir into the juice. Return to the heat and simmer for 2 minutes until clear, stirring all the time. If using potato flour, do *not* let juice boil. The jelly should not be too thick; it resembles syrup when put to set. Pour the jelly into individual serving dishes or a glass bowl and sprinkle a little sugar on top to prevent a skin forming. Scatter halved almonds on top. Serve with milk or cream. *Serves 6–8.*

Acknowledgements

The publishers wish to thank the following organizations and individuals for their help in the preparation of this book: The Danish Cattle and Beef Board; The Danish Dairy Federation; ESS-FOOD Eksport-Svineslagteriernes Salgsforening; The Flour Advisory Bureau and the Royal Greenland Trade Department.

Special thanks are also due to the homo economists who tested the recipes: Jette Kramme Ejlersen, Danish Meat Research Institute; Jytte Nipper, Danish Dairy Federation; Susanne Gallier and Moya Clarke, consultants.

The authors particularly wish to acknowledge the inspiration and help over many years from the Danish cookery book *Mad,* first published in 1909 by Ingeborg Suhr, founder of the Danish college of domestic science which bears her name. They are also indebted to Gyldendal's *Blå Kogebog* for material in chapter one.

If you live in the Bristish Isles and would like further information please write in the first instance to the Danish Dairy Board, Betchworth House, 57-65 Station Road, Redhill, Surrey RH1 1DL or the Danish Bacon and Meat Council, Riveside Centre, 40 High Street, Kingston-upon-Thames, Surrey KT1 1HL.

If you live elsewhere, please write to: Danish Agricultural Marketing Board, Vester Farimagsgade 6, 1606 Copenhagen V, Denmark.

DANWICH is the registered trade mark of The Danish Centre Ltd for Danish open sandwiches.

Index